THOMAS JEFFERSON
MUSICIAN & VIOLINIST

What so hard, so stubborn, or so fierce,

But Music for the Time will change its Nature?

The Man who has not Music in his Soul,

Or is not touch'd with Concord of sweet Sounds,

Is fit for Treasons, Stratagems, & Spoils,

The Motions of his Mind are dull as Night,

And his Affections dark as Erebus:

Let no such Man be trusted.—

— from Thomas Jefferson's
Commonplace Book

These lines are from Jefferson's *Literary Commonplace Book* and were inscribed by Jefferson before 1763. His commonplace book was the volume into which Jefferson, until age 30, copied passages from literature that had particular meaning to him. The source of the quotation originates in Shakespeare as printed in the *Thesaurus Dramaticus*, a collection of excerpts taken from popular British plays that Jefferson very likely used as his immediate source. However, the entire first line and a number of other words in this quotation are Jefferson's own and not the Bard of Avon's. The original Shakepearean language can be found in *The Merchant of Venice*, Act V, scene 1, lines 81 and following. See Douglas L. Wilson, ed., *Jefferson's Literary Commonplace Book* (Princeton: Princeton UP, 1989), 114–115.

THOMAS JEFFERSON
MUSICIAN & VIOLINIST

Sandor Salgo
Professor of Music (Emeritus)
Stanford University

THOMAS JEFFERSON FOUNDATION

Critical support for this work was provided by the Office of the President, Stanford University.

Dear Dr. Casper:

This essay was created because of your love of music and your profound interest in the author of the Declaration of Independence. A further and special link to Mr. Jefferson is your fondness of singing (I hear a fine basso in your voice.) Since you inspired and suggested this essay, it is dedicated to you—leader, educator, lawyer, humanist—a true Jeffersonian.

Christmas, 1998
Stanford, California

ACKNOWLEDGMENTS

When asked after a performance of his Mass why the "Credo" was the longest movement, Stravinsky quipped, "Because there is so much to believe." These acknowledgements are analogous: there are so many people I would like to thank.

Scholarship concerning many aspects of Mr. Jefferson's musical life still advances over terra incognita. I am much indebted to Helen Cripe, Ph.D. for her seminal dissertation and study of the subject and to Professor Ronald R. Kidd of Purdue University, whose suggestions were most helpful.

The superb work of two great Jeffersonian scholars, Professor Merrill D. Peterson—who is blessed with a divine spark for historical narrative—and Dr. Douglas L. Wilson—whose books are models of brilliant and meticulous scholarship—were constant inspirations to me in writing this paper. Dr. Wilson was most gracious and generous with his time in identifying Jefferson's handwriting as well as in suggesting ways to avoid the blind alleys that this topic sometimes presents to those first exploring it.

In preparing this essay, I was most fortunate to have a small circle of close friends who, along with members of my family, acted as benevolent but constructively critical editors, and, moreover, surrounded me with an aura of support and faith in the project. I am deeply indebted to them.

My friend and former Stanford student, Bruce Wolfe, though he chose to designate himself as my "research associate," was in reality infinitely more helpful than the title implies. From suggesting new avenues of research while driving me across the Virginia countryside, to guiding me through the labyrinth of the Library of Congress, to obtaining illustrations, checking footnotes and arranging the text, his efforts were indispensable in the creation of this paper.

Professor Alan Cohen brought to this essay his remarkable organizational skills and his professional psychological insights. Alan also made suggestions for much befitting phraseology. Thanks, too, go to Joan Cohen, for her reading of the manuscript. My friends Starrett and Nancy Dalton read the manuscript several times, making numerous and valuable suggestions for improvement. My wife, Priscilla, was present at the "birth" of this essay and has watched with keen interest every stage of its development; her help has proved, as always, an inestimably important resource for me. My daughter, Deborah Salgo Dranove, lent her considerable editorial and linguistic expertise to give this paper its final shape. Again, my deepest thanks to friends and family.

I would also like to express my gratitude and warm thanks to the following individuals and their institutions for their helpfulness and courtesy: Dr. Daniel P. Jordan, President, Thomas Jefferson Foundation, Inc., Monticello; The International Center for Jefferson Studies, Monticello; Robert E. Belknap, M.D., of Mill Valley, California; Ms. Heather Moore, Rare Books and Special Collections Division at the Alderman Library, and Ms. Jane Edminster Penner, Music Librarian, both at the University of Virginia, Charlottesville; Mr. Clark Evans, Rare Books and Special Collections Division, and Mr. Michael J. Klein, Manuscript Division, both of the Library of Congress, Washington, D.C.; Ms. Sonia H. Moss, Interlibrary Loan Division and Ms. Riva Bacon, Music Librarian, both of Stanford University; my friend, Hans Mueller, for his translation of the passage from Heine; Prof. Edgar Hein of Hamburg, Germany; and the Archbishop Alemany Library of Dominican College, San Rafael, California. Thanks also go to Ms. Priscilla Scott, Ms. Connie Rothermel, Ms.Carolyn Paxton, my student assistant Ms. Tiffany Kuo, and to Ms. Jaqueline B. Wender and Ms. Ingrid Deiwiks (both of the President's Office, Stanford University), and to Herbert Myers, Curator, Rare Instrument Collection, Music Department, Stanford, for the assistance and many courtesies they extended to me. I would also like to thank Gaye Wilson, Monticello Research Department, for valuable assistance in checking data, footnotes, and endless details.

Finally, I want to thank my editor, Dr. James Horn, Saunders Director, The International Center for Jefferson Studies, Monticello, for his many insightful suggestions for improving the manuscript, his editorial expertise and his enthusiasm for this project. It has been a privilege to work with him.

S. S.

PREFACE

As a youth of sixteen in Budapest, Hungary, I was stirred and deeply moved by my first reading of the Declaration of Independence in an amateurish Hungarian translation. It made an even more profound impression upon me some years later in America, when, as an adopted son of this great Republic, I could read this marvelous document in its original language. The sweep and rhythm of the prose, its dignity, the beauty of its cadences—all later reminded me of lines in Keats' poem, "On First Looking Into Chapman's Homer":

Then felt I like some watcher of the skies,
When a new planet swims into his ken.

My admiration for Jefferson continued to grow throughout the years. In a rehearsal of Mozart's orchestral music at a Richmond, Virginia college just after World War II, I had the good fortune to meet Dumas Malone, the great Jeffersonian scholar, who coincidentally loved the music of Mozart. Professor Malone informed me that Mr. Jefferson, for all his literary skills, was also an accomplished violinist.

This revelation struck a sympathetic chord within me, since I was trained as a concert violinist and conductor. After studies on violin with Jeno Hubay, then conducting with Fritz Busch, I came to America in 1939 as a member of the Roth String Quartet. I joined the faculty of Westminster Choir College, directed chamber music performances at Princeton University, and, at the same time, studied conducting with George Szell in New York City. In 1949 I moved west with my wife, Priscilla, to begin a long and happy association with Stanford University. Somewhat concurrently (from 1956 to 1992), I served as the Music Director of The Carmel Bach Festival and, in addition, conducted the symphony orchestra of Marin County, California. Because of academic and professional commitments, my interest in Jefferson lay dormant. It took the encouragement and support of Dr. Gerhard Casper, President of Stanford University, to rekindle this interest and set me on the road to further investigation.

S. S.

INTRODUCTION

Thomas Jefferson was a man of many talents. Indeed, the sheer multiplicity of his talents has always been a hallmark of his distinction. President John F. Kennedy famously told an audience of Nobel Prize winners that their collective presence represented the greatest assembly of talent in the White House since Thomas Jefferson dined alone. This multi-talented man was, of course, one of the key founders of the American republic, but even before conclusion of the Revolutionary war, a French savant who visited him at Monticello would describe him for European readers as "an American, who, without ever having quitted his own country, is Musician, Draftsman, Surveyor, Astronomer, Natural Philosopher, Jurist, and Statesman." Nearly one hundred years later, the American biographer James Parton formulated his own litany of Jefferson's talents, characterizing him as a man who "could calculate an eclipse, survey an estate, tie an artery, plan an edifice, try a cause, break a horse, dance a minuet, and play the violin."* But while Jefferson's talents as a musician have been long recognized, as these remarks indicate, they have received relatively little appreciation or attention. This has been especially true of his career as a violinist—until now.

Jefferson's remarkable life and career have been studied in detail by historians and biographers, but the author of the original essay presented here comes at his subject from a different perspective. Prof. Sandor Salgo is a professionally trained musician and teacher, long associated with Stanford University, and for many years an acclaimed conductor. Like Jefferson himself, his instrument is the violin, and his knowledge of that instrument is not only technical but deeply historical as well. He thus brings to the subject of Jefferson the musician and violinist a broad understanding of the history of music, its forms and conventions in Jefferson's day, including a detailed knowledge of the literature and artistry of the violin. This is shown to be essential if we are to see and understand Jefferson's musicianship in an authentic historical context.

It needs to be emphasized that music and musicianship were important matters for Jefferson. Although he referred to music as a "delightful recreation," it was far from a casual or peripheral concern. About his personal feelings and emotions, he was notoriously guarded and protective; consequently, his inner life is a subject that has largely defied the best efforts of most biographers. But his undisguised passion for music offers a rare point of entry, for music, he once confessed, "is the favorite passion of my soul." What prompted this disclosure

---

* James Parton, *Life of Thomas Jefferson* (Boston, 1874), 165.

was the need to explain to a European correspondent his sense of extreme deprivation: "fortune has cast my lot in a country where [music] is in a state of deplorable barbarism." For one who was constitutionally positive and optimistic, especially where the character of his country was concerned, this is a telling confession indeed. But as Prof. Salgo amply demonstrates, this is a consistent theme in Jefferson's writings, and for this reason music assumes a special importance.

It is Prof. Salgo's specialized knowledge that enabled him to investigate, as no one has ever done previously, the character and principal elements of Jefferson's musicianship. We have long known, for example, what books Jefferson had in his monumental library on music and on the art of the violin. And thanks to such scholars as Dumas Malone and Merrill D. Peterson, we have long recognized that Jefferson tended to draw his knowledge directly from his reading. But it remained for Prof. Salgo to provide the needed catalyst and to demonstrate, in concrete terms, the ways in which Jefferson's books informed his musicianship and, in particular, his playing as a violinist. But Prof. Salgo's investigation was more wide-ranging than this. Following leads developed by Helen Cripe and Ronald R. Kidd, he sought out and explored the myriad documents pertaining to music in the various Jeffersonian archives. He was thus able to portray the role of music in Jefferson's family life, including the musicianship of his wife and his daughters, and to consider the significance of the Jefferson family's extensive collection of musical scores. Perhaps most impressively, by skillfully assessing the violin literature Jefferson was familiar with and the levels at which he engaged it, the author is able to give a truly fresh and revealing account of a neglected but important aspect of Jefferson's experience.

It was my good fortune to have welcomed Prof. Salgo to Monticello's International Center for Jefferson Studies some years ago. He was at an early stage of his project, and the Center was seeking, then as now, to lend encouragement and support to scholars of Jefferson's life and times. It seemed clear to us even then, as we attempted to offer such assistance as we could, that the subject and the student were superlatively well matched. This has now been gratifyingly borne out. There are, understandably, those who remain skeptical that new and important light can be shed on so familiar and well-studied a subject as Thomas Jefferson, but readers of this fine essay hold in their hands incontrovertible proof that it can still be done.

— *Douglas L. Wilson*

To this day, 175 years after his death, Thomas Jefferson has remained one of America's most beloved and admired historical personalities. In addition to his peerless political contributions as statesman and as one of the Founding Fathers of our country, Jefferson has been widely recognized for works of enduring importance in such diverse fields as architecture, science, political philosophy, law, literature, and agriculture. What is perhaps less well known, however, is Jefferson's love and talent for music and musical performance, especially violin playing. Most Jeffersonian scholars have devoted no more than a few lines in their biographies and critical studies to the vital role that music and the violin played in his life. This writer's goal is to attempt to illuminate another facet of this amazing man, in particular his accomplishments as musician and violinist.

As Merrill D. Peterson, the great Jeffersonian scholar, has felicitously observed, while the author of the Declaration of Independence had "an effortless talent for drawing men to him, he was nonetheless a man of almost impenetrable emotional reserve."[1] Despite this reticence, from a few direct and many peripheral sources there emerges an image of a man deeply committed to music and to his instrument—the violin. In this essay we shall explore his love of and skill in playing this queen of eighteenth-century instruments, as well as the variety of musical experiences which delighted him throughout his life.

JEFFERSON'S EARLY MUSICAL EXPERIENCES

The central, hilly part of Virginia was wilderness country when Thomas Jefferson was born on April 13, 1743, in his family's home of Shadwell near the village of Charlottesville. His father, Peter Jefferson, a surveyor, was a self-made man and very much respected in Albemarle County. With native ability, hard work, and business acumen he managed to secure sizable acreage to support his wife and their ten children, eight of whom survived infancy. He was a man of great physical strength who was interested in his eldest son, Tom, and in Tom's education. Tom adored him. Jefferson family lore holds that by his sixth birthday Tom had read every book in his father's library.

Thomas, both as a boy and later the man, was largely silent about his mother, Jane Randolph Jefferson. The Randolphs have been called (although not convincingly proven to

---

[1] Merrill D. Peterson, introduction to *The Portable Thomas Jefferson* (New York: Viking-Penguin, 1975), xii. Please see the bibliography at the end of this essay for a full listing of sources consulted.

be) descendants of a king of Scotland and were among the first families of Virginia. Later on, being a Randolph must have opened many doors for young Jefferson in Virginia society. But Thomas was not impressed by his Scottish genealogy—then or later—for he did not care for kings.

There is no indication that his parents were musically inclined. The musical impulse and encouragement to play the violin seems to have come from Thomas' older sister, Jane, who had a lovely singing voice. The two often performed together, Jane singing and her brother accompanying her on his violin. Thomas was especially fond of listening to her sing Psalms.[2]

We know nothing about the boy's first instruction on the violin. However, we do know that when, as a nine-year-old, he became a boarding student at the Reverend William Douglas' Latin School, he could play the violin while reading music, or "play by the book," as it was then expressed.[3] His father's death in 1757 traumatized the young Jefferson;[4] he is said to have immersed himself in his studies and his violin as a way of assuaging his grief.[5] In the same year, at age fourteen, he entered the loghouse school of the redoubtable Reverend James Maury. Thomas was by then considered an accomplished violinist.

Before Peter Jefferson died, he is said to have expressed the wish that his son Thomas receive a good classical education. Thus, in 1760, after finishing his work at Reverend Maury's, the young man enrolled in the College of William and Mary, some 150 miles from Shadwell, at the colonial capital, Williamsburg.

In those days Williamsburg had a straight main street—the Duke of Gloucester Street—three quarters of a mile long, with the Capitol and the College at opposite ends, and about two hundred houses, a collection of shops, a parish church, and a tavern. It was a sleepy little town of perhaps 1800 people when the law courts and the legislature, the House of Burgesses, were not in session. During the spring and fall "Publick Times," when the law courts were rendering justice and the Burgesses were in session, Williamsburg was jammed with visitors:

For then... the Taverns, Inns, Publick Houses, Ordinaries, private Dwellings, and nearby Plantations were filled to overflowing.... [6]

---

[2] Willard Sterne Randall, *Jefferson: A Life* (New York: Holt, 1993), 16.

[3] Dumas Malone, *Jefferson and His Time*, 6 vols., (Boston: Little, Brown, 1948–1981), vol. 1, *Jefferson the Virginian*, 48.

[4] Thomas Jefferson to Thomas Jefferson Randolph, 24 Nov. 1808, in Edwin Morris Betts and James Adam Bear, Jr., eds. *The Family Letters of Thomas Jefferson* (Charlottesville: Virginia UP, 1966), 362-3.

[5] W.S. Randall, *Jefferson: A Life*, 16, 18.

[6] Jane Carson, *Colonial Virginians at Play* (Charlottesville: Colonial Williamsburg, Inc., 1965), 195–96, quoting Rutherfoord Goodwin, *A Brief & True Report Concerning Williamsburg in Virginia* (3rd edn., Williamsburg, 1941), 35–7.

Musical and theatrical performances flourished.[7]

While a student at William and Mary for two years, Thomas was industrious and eager to learn but dissatisfied with the quality of the faculty, except for one man, Dr. William Small, a gifted Professor of Mathematics from Scotland. Small was a man of vast learning, especially well-grounded in science, mathematics and philosophy. Noting the ability and interest of the zealous, red-haired student, Dr. Small not only gave Jefferson an extra measure of his time but also his friendship. Small was well acquainted with the rapidly expanding horizons of science and interested in imparting some of his wide knowledge to his eager student. His teaching fell on fertile ground: Small's scientific outlook and rational approach to problem-solving stayed with Jefferson all his life. More than half a century later he was still acknowledging his intellectual debt to Dr. Small.[8]

It seems clear that at that time in Jefferson's life, music—and especially the violin—were high priorities for him. For example, during Christmas, 1760, at Colonel Nathaniel Dandridge's house in Hanover County, he met a young Virginian, classmate, and fellow violinist, one Patrick Henry. The house resounded with the music of violins all during the holiday.[9] John Page, Jefferson's classmate and closest college friend, provided another testament to Jefferson's interest in the violin. He said that while other William and Mary students were hunting, fishing, and gaming, Jefferson would stay in his room studying and, very likely, practicing his violin.[10]

However studious he may have been, the young man was not long immune to the attractions of the fairer sex. Soon after he completed his studies at William and Mary in 1762, Jefferson fell headlong in love with sixteen year-old Rebecca Burwell, the orphaned daughter of a distinguished plantation owner. But, even while fairly consumed by the pangs of love, the violin was not far from his mind. On January 20, 1763, while visiting at the family home in Shadwell, he wrote a letter to John Page, and in it he first indulged in a post-adolescent fantasy about "sailing up the river again in a full-rigged flat" (a boat he was then actually building) and, later, how he would expand the voyage:

---

[7] Same.

[8] In his 1821 Autobiography, Jefferson wrote, "It was my great good fortune, and what probably fixed the destinies of my life, that Dr. Wm. Small of Scotland, was then Professor of Mathematics, a man profound in most of the useful branches of science, with a happy talent of communication, correct and gentlemanly manners, & an enlarged & liberal mind." *Autobiography of Thomas Jefferson, 1743-1790 together with a Summary of the Chief Events in Jefferson's Life,* Paul Leicester Ford, ed., (New York: Putnam, 1914), 3–4.

[9] Thomas Jefferson to William Wirt, 5 Aug. 1815.

[10] W.S. Randall, *Jefferson: A Life,* 41, from "John Page's Autobiography" (Virginia Historical Register, July, 1850), 151.

Have you an inclination to travel, Page? Because if you have I shall be glad of your compa-
ny. For you must know that as soon as the Rebecca (the name I intend to give the vessel
above mentioned) is completely finished I intend to hoist sail and away. I shall visit partic-
*ularly England Holland France Spain Italy (**where I would buy me a good fiddle**) and*
Egypt and return through the British provinces to the northward home. This, to be sure,
would take us two or three years and if we should not both be cured of love in that time I
think the Devil would be in it.[11]

Five years and five months later Jefferson found the "good fiddle" he was looking for—
but in Williamsburg, not Italy. He paid Dr. William Pasteur, a medical doctor and apothe-
cary shop owner with business premises on the Duke of Gloucester Street, five British pounds
for it.[12]

The Lawyer-musician

In the upper levels of Virginia society, and more particularly at Williamsburg in the latter half of the eighteenth century, a gentleman was expected among other things to be an
accomplished horseman and competent swordsman. In addition, he was expected to be a
good dancer and to play a musical instrument with skill. Although it was not considered
dignified for a gentleman to play a wind instrument, the violin was highly regarded. There
were few harpsichords or pianos.

Because of the importance it attached to dancing, Virginia plantation society employed
highly esteemed itinerant dancing and music masters who provided instruction in social
dancing. Most, if not all, dancing lessons and "assemblies" (i.e., dancing events) were accompanied by fiddlers.[13] Norman Arthur Benson, in his pioneering study, describes the activities

---

[11] Julian P. Boyd, ed., et al., *The Papers of Thomas Jefferson*, 27 vols. to date, (Princeton: Princeton UP, 1950–1999), 1:7, 8; [hereafter cited as *Papers*]. [Emphasis supplied]

[12] James Adams Bear, Jr., and Lucia C. Stanton, eds, *Jefferson's Memorandum Books: Accounts, with Legal Records and Miscellany, 1767-1826*, 2 vols. (Princeton, NJ: Princeton UP, 1997), 1:77; hereafter cited as "*Memorandum & Account Books.*" This instrument could well have been the one Jefferson later called his "Cremona." See the fol-lowing note for a discussion of the meaning of the term "fiddle." See also n. 108 below.

[13] A "fiddle" (ultimately from the Latin *vitulari*, "celebrate a festival," "to be joyful") is "[a] stringed instrument of the violin family; spec[ifically] a violin." Its current usage is chiefly derogatory and/or colloquial. *New Shorter Oxford English Dictionary* (Oxford: Clarendon Press, 1973), 1:941. "Colloquially, 'fiddle' is used for a member of the violin family or for the 'kit'... ." Mary Remnant, "Fiddle," *The New GROVE Dictionary of Music and Musicians*®, Sadie Stanley, ed., 20 vols. (London: MacMillan, 1980), 6:527–33; hereafter cited as *New Grove Dictionary*. Typically, fiddlers hold the instrument in the left hand in the manner of violinists but place it lower on the chest rather than between the chin and collarbone. In Jefferson's world, there was a considerable differ-

of a number of these music masters who were practicing their art in eighteenth-century Virginia, among them Charles and Mary Stagg, William Dering, and Stephen Tence.[14] These dancing masters typically had large classes assembled for them as they moved from one plantation to another.

Dancing was important in Jefferson's social life. John Harvie, executor of Jefferson's father's estate, paid a Mr. Inglis, a dancing master, a fee for six months' instruction for Thomas and his four sisters while Thomas was still a student of Reverend Maury's.[15] A few years later, on the evening of October 6, 1763, had we been present at the Raleigh Tavern in Williamsburg, we might have glimpsed the strikingly tall and very ardent Jefferson as he danced with the object of his unrequited affection, Miss Rebecca Burwell.[16]

After completing his studies at William and Mary in 1762, Jefferson had to decide upon

---

ence in the content of music performed between country fiddlers who generally improvised popular tunes, jigs, reels, and similar music at dances and parties (often using an open string as a drone and employing modal scales and playing in first position and without vibrato) and violinists who, like Jefferson, performed art music from printed and manuscript scores. Indeed, Jefferson has been accused, along with Patrick Henry, by an unnamed "early authority" as being "the worst fiddler in the colony." Helen Cripe, *Thomas Jefferson and Music* (Charlottesville: UP of Virginia, 1974), 88-9. Ms. Cripe correctly points out (89, n.5) that art music would have sounded out of tune to a person accustomed only to country fiddling. Jefferson, however, when purchasing new strings for his violins, nearly always referred to them in his memorandum and account books as "fiddlestrings." See *Memorandum & Account Books,* ("fiddlestrings") 1:70, 82, 147, 205, 209, 210, 257, 419, 569, 2:876; ("violin strings") 1:403, and 2:907.

[14] Norman Arthur Benson, "The Itinerant Dancing and Music Masters of Eighteenth Century America," (Ph.D. diss., Univ. of Minnesota, 1963), 47-57. The Staggs were much sought-after teachers in Williamsburg. After instruction, everyone—including adults—joined the dance. There were many formal balls. Jane Carson mentions Philip Fithian, a teacher of the children of the fabulously wealthy Robert Carter at his plantation, "Nomini Hall," attended a ball at Colonel Richard Lee's residence ("Lee Hall") that lasted from Monday through Thursday. Then, with customary hospitality, the Colonel invited the guests to stay another day. Fithian was impressed by the luxuriant affair, the sumptuous dinner, the elegance of the ladies whose dresses of silk and brocades rustled behind them as they danced minuets, reels, country dances, and jigs according to that order and as taught by the dancing masters. Carson, 22–3.

[15] Malone, 1:47.

[16] See W.S. Randall, *Jefferson: A Life,* 58–65. It was not merely a young lady's looks that attracted Jefferson's attention among the many examples of socially prominent young womanhood that he encountered while in Williamsburg. In a letter to his friend, Will Fleming (*Papers,* 1:12–13) and believed to have been written in October, 1763: "…. Last Saturday I left Ned Carter's where I had been happy in other good company, but particularly that of Miss Jenny Taliaferro: and though I can view the beauties of this world with the most philosophical indifference, I could not but be sensible of the justice of the character you had given me of her. She has in my opinion a great resemblance of Nancy Wilton, but prettier. I was vastly pleased with her playing on the spinnette [sic] and singing, and could not help calling to mind those sublime verses of the Cumberland genius

"Oh! how I was charmed to see
Orpheus' music all in thee."

FIGURE 1. *George Wythe (Courtesy Library of Virginia)*

a profession. To follow his natural inclination toward science, architecture—even music—was simply not possible for him because, in those days, there were no viable careers in those areas. The study of law seemed to suit Jefferson; however, there were no law schools at that time. As luck would have it, Dr. Small introduced him to George Wythe (pronounced *with*), an eminent teacher of jurisprudence and one of the most highly respected lawyers in the American colonies. Jefferson quickly accepted apprenticeship in Wythe's office and began the formal study of the law.

The tall, lanky legal assistant was happy in his new situation. Jefferson worked five years with Wythe, who, like Dr. Small, became the young man's friend and mentor.

"The Sage of Virginia," as Wythe became known, was a lawyer with profound knowledge of the language and literature of the ancient Greek and Roman authors as well as of the entire spectrum of English and French legal commentary.[17] He opened new intellectual vistas for Jefferson, while the latter served as Wythe's legal apprentice and disciple.

Wythe took his apprentice to the Governor's Palace in Williamsburg to meet the Royal Governor, Francis Fauquier (locally pronounced *fáwk-yer*), an Englishman appointed by the Crown. Fauquier was cultivated, urbane, and popular with Virginians. They even named one of the Virginia Colony's counties after him. According to Jefferson, he was an admirable violinist.[18] The Governor must have thought highly of the young law student's playing because he invited him to be a member of his weekly chamber music group. Fauquier or John Randolph played first violin; Jefferson probably played second. The others in the ensemble, also leaders in Virginia society, were good players as well: Robert Carter, an extraordinarily wealthy and influential plantation owner, played harpsichord; John Tyler, Jefferson's good friend, junior William and Mary classmate and, later, fellow law apprentice, played cello.[19]

---

[17] Jefferson, *Autobiography,* 6. Jefferson therein referred to Wythe as his "faithful and beloved Mentor in youth, and most affectionate friend through life." Wythe was one of the signers of the Declaration of Independence.

[18] Thomas Jefferson to L.H. Girardin, 15 Jan. 1815; original letter in Library of Congress

[19] There is evidence that Jefferson also tried his hand at playing the cello. See, e.g., entry for "strings for violoncello" in *Memorandum & Account Books,* 1:29.

John Tyler later became Governor of Virginia and an important figure in American politics, as well as the father of a future President. Tyler and Jefferson practiced on their instruments together and, as stated, played at Governor Fauquier's soirées. Tyler must have been quite a fine cellist because he aroused the good-hearted envy of Jefferson, who reportedly commented that if he possessed Tyler's bow arm, he, Jefferson, "would yield the palm to no man living in excellence of performance!"[20] We don't know the exact contents of Governor Fauquier's music library, but we can reasonably surmise that it included Haydn quartets, Corelli and Vivaldi sonatas and concerti grossi, and other pieces by European and English composers that were then available for purchase in London, an important center of music publishing.

Much later in life, in his 1821 *Autobiography*, Jefferson would recall the profound and inspiring postprandial conversations within this triumvirate of exceptional men—Small, Wythe and Fauquier.[21] Discussions ranged over philosophy, science, the arts, politics, and much more. For Jefferson, the experiences of those evenings were unforgettable and irreplaceable. We can infer that these three gave Jefferson an education that helped lay the foundation for much of his transcendent knowledge, penetrating political insight, and extraordinary gifts in expressing himself in writing.

At this time Jefferson also developed a fondness for musical theater. His account books provide evidence that he attended numerous Williamsburg performances of the Virginia Company of Comedians as well as those of the American Theater Company. While Jefferson was apparently interested in all genres of theatrical performance, his particular favorite then was the English ballad opera, exemplified by works such as Thomas Arne's *Thomas and Sally* and *Love in a Village* and John Gay's celebrated *The Beggar's Opera*. This genre is based on spoken dialogue with songs and dances of familiar as well as original music; it became extremely popular in England and the colonies in the eighteenth century.

In his personal experiences with English ballad operas, Jefferson undoubtedly made the acquaintance of Peter Pelham, a London-born organist, conductor, and teacher. According to his memorandum and account books, Jefferson attended many of Pelham's musical performances, including musical theater. Pelham had immigrated to America from England in his youth and was one of the most outstanding American musicians of his time. He was first

---

[20] Lyon G. Tyler, *The Letters and Times of the Tylers*, 2 vols. (Richmond: Whittet & Shepperson, 1884-96), 1:54-55. By "palm" Jefferson meant, "the reward of honor due a victor," from *The Random House Dictionary of the English Language* ed. Jess Stein (New York: Random House, 1966).

[21] Jefferson, *Autobiography*, 6.

employed as an organist in Boston, finally (about 1754) settling in as organist and harpsichordist of the Bruton Parish Church in Williamsburg.[22]

The violin continued to play an important role in Jefferson's daily life as he began to practice law and travel out of Williamsburg on legal matters for his clients. He bought a "kit violin" (or, simply, "kit"), a small instrument with an extremely soft sound used frequently by the dancing masters. Jefferson, ever the innovator, designed a handsome but practical case for the instrument, so it could easily be attached to his saddle.[23] The kit enabled him to practice in whatever room he had to spend the night without the risk of disturbing others.[24]

Music and the Master of Monticello

In 1769 Jefferson, a full-fledged practicing lawyer, was elected to the Virginia House of Burgesses. In this same year he began to realize his long-held dream of building a Roman-style villa on property a few miles south of Charlottesville that had been part of his share of his father's estate. The property was dominated by a small mountain, and was given its Italian name, Monticello, by Jefferson. His classical orientation led him to books containing designs

---

[22] Cripe, 6. Peter Pelham is also mentioned in a non-musical context in the *Memorandum & Account Books*, 1:34. To make ends meet, he, like so many musicians then (as well as today), was obliged by his financial circumstances to take additional "day jobs," some of which for Pelham were serving as clerk to the Governor and to a committee of the Burgesses, as well as town Jailer (!).

[23] In the "Nicholas Trist Memorandum," Jefferson is quoted and refers to his "kit" in these words: "At first I carried about with me that little instrument which I've given to Lewis…", Henry Stephens Randall, *The Life of Thomas Jefferson*, 3 vols., (New York: Derby & Jackson, 1858. Repr. New York: Da Capo Press, 1972), 1:131, hereafter cited as "H.S. Randall, *The Life of Thomas Jefferson*". Mr. Trist was Jefferson's grandson-in-law, married to Jefferson's granddaughter Virginia Randolph. His "memorandum" consists of verbatim notes of a conversation he had with Mr. Jefferson in March, 1826, when the patriarch was nearly 83 years of age.

[24] The origin of the name of the instrument is unclear. Some scholars relate it to the Greek "Kithara," while others think of it as a "kitten" to the larger violin. Because of its pocket size, the French called it *pochette*. Italians named it *sordino*, suggesting its muted sound. Germans, expressing its most common usage, called it *Tanzmeistergeige*. These curious instruments were made from the sixteenth to the nineteenth centuries. Throughout its history, the kit violin went through a number of shapes: from boat-shaped and pear-shaped, to close to the shape of our present-day violin. From the seventeenth century on, kits had elongated necks and very small, narrow bodies, which sometimes were inlaid with precious materials, like one made by Genova and on display in the Royal College of Music, London. The illustrious Antonio Stradivari made several kit violins in different shapes. The kit's tuning was in fifths, like present-day violins, occasionally an octave higher. Kits came with or without a soundpost, an internal piece of narrow dowel placed near the bridge that greatly amplifies any string instrument's natural sound. In a kit violin, the presence of a soundpost means a small but agreeable tone and was, therefore, most often used by the dancing masters of Jefferson's time. The kit without a soundpost is almost inaudible to those other than the player, See James W. McKinnon, "Kit," *New Grove Dictionary*, 10: 85–8.

of the renowned Italian Renaissance architect, Andrea Palladio, whose ideas guided him in the construction of his home.

In the following year he suffered the catastrophic loss of his extensive library—together with almost all his music—in a fire at the family home at Shadwell. The only positive thing to come from the event was that "Old Isaac," a family slave, rescued Jefferson's violin from the flames. Much of the pain of his misfortune was soon offset, however, by a more auspicious occurrence: he became acquainted with Martha Wayles Skelton, an attractive widow with many suitors. She played the harpsichord, the guitar, and sang. According to Jefferson family tradition, Jefferson's violin playing and pleasant singing voice won Martha's heart; conversely, Martha's harpsichord playing and singing must have made a reciprocal mark on Thomas.[25] It was their playing and singing together that contributed to Jefferson's success in courting her. There is a tradition that during their courtship two hopeful dandies arrived at her doorway simultaneously. First they heard Martha and Thomas playing the harpsi-

FIGURE 2. *Two eighteenth-century English kit violins on either side of a standard-sized 18th century violin of German origin. Note that the necks of all three instruments are of almost identical length. The kit violin on the left is "gamba" or viol-shaped and made by Betts (John?), London, late 18th century. The kit violin on the right is an English violin-shaped kit also of late 18th century construction. (Courtesy of Herbert Myers, Curator, the Harry R. Lange Historical Collection of Musical Instruments and Books, Stanford University.)*

---

[25] The magnetic effects of another musically-inclined young lady had already induced currents of admiration within Jefferson. See n. 16, above.

chord and violin together, but when they heard them sing in beautiful harmony they turned and left.[26]

After a two-year courtship, Martha and Thomas were married on New Year's Day, 1772, a festive occasion accompanied by fiddling, dancing, and singing that lasted for several days. One of the bride's wedding presents from her new husband was a costly "Forte-piano…worthy the acceptance of a lady for whom I intend it" that he had ordered from his agent in London months earlier in a letter expressing great urgency.[27] Afterwards, Jefferson took his bride to Monticello, then under construction. Indeed, Mrs. Jefferson, whom her husband came to call "Patty", spent the rest of her life in a residence under constant construction.

Not long after he and his new wife took up residence at Monticello, Jefferson invited an Italian immigrant violinist-harpsichordist, Signor Francis Alberti to settle in Charlottesville for the express purpose of giving music lessons to him and his wife. There can be little doubt that Alberti was a product of a tradition of violin performance as practiced in Italy and that he attempted to communicate Italian performance practice to Jefferson. For his part, Jefferson developed a deep regard for Signor Alberti, and studied with him for several years.[28] More than fifty years later, Jefferson told his 26-year-old grandson-in law, Nicholas Trist, that he "suppos[ed]" that he practiced the violin "no less than *three hours* a day" for a "dozen years."[29] Given even only half as much practice per day (the alleged three hours discounted by half, given a fairly presumable limitation on the patriarch's powers of precise recollection) his professional instruction and his customary degree of concentration and intellectual intensity, it seems probable to this writer that Jefferson developed considerable mastery of the violin.

---

[26] H.S. Randall, *The Life of Thomas Jefferson,* 1:64.

[27] Thomas Jefferson to Thomas Adams, 1 June 1771, addressed to Mr. Adams and "to be left at Nando's Coffee house Fleet-street, London." *Papers*, 1:71–2. Curiously, on April 29, 1779 the Forte-piano seems to have been sold to General Friedrich von Riedesel, a captured and paroled Hessian officer living near Monticello, for £100. *Memorandum & Account Books*, 1:478. See also the same, 1:477 n. 36.

[28] Alberti, a native of Faenza, Italy, taught music at Williamsburg and was apparently persuaded by Jefferson to come to Albermale County. "Over a period of several years he gave [Jefferson] violin lessons and taught music to Martha and [Randolph Jefferson] and probably other members of the Shadwell and Monticello households." Alberti died at Richmond in 1785. *Memorandum & Account Books,* 1:70, n.61.

[29] Emphasis in original. Quoted in H.S. Randall, *The Life of Thomas Jefferson,* 1:131. Nicholas Trist, Memorandum, March 22, 1826, reproduced in part in H.S. Randall, 1:131–132; now kept in the Library of Congress, Washington, D.C. Mr. Trist quotes Mr. Jefferson as saying "[A]t the breaking out of the Revolution, I laid aside my violin, and have never taken it up again." H.S. Randall, *The Life of Thomas Jefferson*, 1:131. Randall interpreted these remarks by writing, "Mr. Jefferson is not to be understood literally that he never took up his violin again…. He means that he ceased to make it a part of his daily and regular occupation; for he certainly continued to play, occasionally, for his own diversion, or that of others, until his right wrist was broken past (full) recovery, in France." H.S. Randall, *The Life of Thomas Jefferson,* 1:132.

According to his slave, Isaac, the "Old Master… kept three fiddles; played in the arternoons [sic] and sometimes arter [sic] supper." Jefferson also loved to sing. He had a "fine clear voice," and "always singing when ridin' or walkin' ".[30]

Apparently, songs and musical sounds made by keyboard instruments and the violin were constantly audible throughout the Jefferson home at Monticello in the 1770s. A harpsichord was always in the parlor and Mrs. Jefferson played it frequently. These sounds were mingled with the laughter and good-natured shrieks of the couple's children. But to Jefferson's inexpressible grief, only two of their six children, Martha and Mary ("Maria"), attained adulthood.

Martha, the oldest and her mother's name-sake, was known in the family as "Patsy," and

FIGURE 3. *Martha ("Patsy") Jefferson at age 17 by Joseph Boze, oil on ivory, (Courtesy Diplomatic Reception Rooms, United States Department of State, photographed by Will Brown)*

she alone of the children survived her father. Jefferson supervised her strict regimen of education, a significant part of which was harpsichord studies.[31] When she grew up, she

---

[30] James Adams Bear, Jr., ed., *Jefferson at Monticello*, contains "Memoirs of a Monticello Slave" [as dictated to Charles Campbell in the 1840s by Isaac Jefferson] and Hamilton W. Pierson, "The Private Life of Thomas Jefferson," (Charlottesville: UP of Virginia, 1967), 13.

[31] In letters to his daughter Martha, Jefferson did not hesitate to prescribe a daily routine of study, with music being an important component. For example:

"With respect to the distribution of your time the following is what I should approve.

 from 8. to 10 oclock practise music.

 from 10. to 1. dance one day and draw another

 from 1. to 2. draw on the day you dance, and write a letter the next day.

 from 3. to 4. read French

 from 4. to 5 excercise yourself in music

 from 5. till bedtime read English, write &c."

Thomas Jefferson (Annapolis) to Martha Jefferson (Philadelphia), 28 Nov. 1783, Edwin Morris Betts and James Adam Bear, Jr., eds. *The Family Letters of Thomas Jefferson*, 19. Seven and a half years later, a few months after his daughter had married, Jefferson wrote her: "…Do not neglect your music. It will be a companion which will sweeten many hours of life to you." Thomas Jefferson (New York) to Martha Jefferson Randolph 4 Apr 1790, same, 51.

greatly resembled him, tall and lean, a good conversationalist and an excellent musician.[32]

Maria, also called "Polly" by her father and sister, was different. Although Jefferson provided her with a good musical education, securing harpsichord lessons for her with John Christopher Moller, the best harpsichord teacher in Philadelphia, Polly's heart was not in her musical studies, nor was she physically up to regular practice. She was Patsy's junior by six years, and it would have been almost unnatural if she had not felt at least some jealousy toward her older and very accomplished sister. Happiness came into her life in 1797 at age nineteen, when she married John Wayles Eppes. However, her joy was not lasting. She died at age twenty-five from complications of childbirth, leaving two children, one infant having previously died.

While music was a fundamental component of the Virginia gentry's social life, for Jefferson it was much more; it seemed an inner necessity, perhaps the focal point of his being. Isaac, the famous Monticello slave, commented that Mr. Jefferson hummed constantly as he worked about the plantation. And there are Jefferson's statements in letters that music was a "delightful recreation"[33] and "the favorite passion of my soul."[34] The latter seems closer to his true feelings. He used music in times of sadness (e.g., a death in the family) to repair his soul or in times of joy (e.g., his wedding) to delight his senses.

A most telling insight into Jefferson's commitment to music is to be found in a letter he wrote four years before his wife's death in 1782. Jefferson was in Williamsburg, serving in the legislature of Revolutionary War-convulsed Virginia. This letter is unique among Jefferson's correspondence because of its outspoken (for Jefferson) expression of his feelings about music,

---

[32] In 1792, Martha ("Patsy") Jefferson married Thomas Mann Randolph, Jr., son of a close friend of her father's. She bore Mr. Randolph eleven children. These proved to be a delight for her father in his old age. After Jefferson's retirement from public life she moved back to Monticello with her family, where she ran the household, was hostess to the many visitors (there were many—often 26 to 30 people for dinner), educated her children, and kept a watchful and tender eye on her adoring father. A truly remarkable woman! Her daughter, Ellen, later wrote, "My mother inherited his [i.e., her father Thomas Jefferson's] taste and talent for music. I have heard persons play with more execution on the piano than she did, but none with more feeling and expression." Coolidge, Ellen Wayles Randolph, Manuscript Notebook of comments on H.S. Randall's biography of Thomas Jefferson, Ellen Coolidge Letterbook, Special Collections, "Jefferson–Coolidge Family," Mss. 9090, n.d., 37.

[33] Letter from Thomas Jefferson to Nathaniel Burwell, Esq., 14 March 1818, Jefferson, *Thomas Jefferson: Writings*, ed. Merrill D. Peterson (New York: The Library of America, 1984) 1412. The words are part of a number of suggestions Jefferson was making on the topic of female education. The context of the quote is: "Music is invaluable where a person has an ear. Where they have not, it should not be attempted. It furnishes *a delightful recreation* for the hours of respite from the cares of the day, and lasts us through life. The taste of this country, too, calls for this accomplishment more strongly than for either of the others [i.e., dancing and drawing]." [Emphasis supplied.]

[34] See the letter to Giovanni Fabbroni quoted following the next paragraph in the body of the text of this monograph.

where the word "passion" (see bold text in quoted material below) appears twice in relation to the subject. The addressee was Giovanni Fabbroni, a young Italian friend of Philip Mazzei, Jefferson's Italian friend and neighbor. Fabbroni was living in Paris at the time. The letter begins with Jefferson discussing at length the course of the Revolutionary War and estimating British casualties, and then moves to music:

> .... *If there is a gratification which I envy any people in this world it is to your country its music. This is the **favorite passion of my soul**, and fortune has cast my lot in a country where it is in a state of deplorable barbarism .... The bounds of an American fortune will not admit the indulgence of a domestic band of musicians. Yet I have thought that a **passion for music** might be reconciled with that oeconomy [sic] which we are obliged to observe. I retain for instance among my domestic servants a gardener (Ortolano), weaver (Tessitore di lino e lano), a cabinet maker (Stipettaio) and a stonecutter (scalpellino lavorante in piano) to which I would add a Vigneron. In a country where, like yours, music is cultivated and practised [sic] by every class of men I suppose there might be found persons of those trades who could perform on the French horn, clarinet or hautboy [i.e., oboe] and bassoon, so that one might have a band of two French horns, two clarinets and hautboys and a bassoon, without enlarging their domestic expences [sic]. A certainty of employment for a half dozen years, and at the end of that time to find them if they chose it a conveyance to their own country might induce them to come here on reasonable wages. Without meaning to give you trouble, perhaps it might be practicable for you in your ordinary intercourse with your people to find out such men disposed to come to America. Sobriety and good nature would be desireable [sic] parts of their characters. If you think such a plan practicable, and will be so kind as to inform me what will be necessary to be done on my part, I will take care that it shall be done. The necessary expences, when informed of them, I can remit before they are wanting, to any port in France with which country alone we have safe correspondence.*
>
> *I am Sir with much esteem your humble servt., T.J.*[35]

Jefferson's interest in and discussion of the hiring of musician-servants suggests an emulation of European aristocracy on the model of the famous Hungarian Prince Nicolaus ("The Magnificent") Eszterházy, who used musician-servants as performers in his excellent eighteenth-century orchestra. That ensemble was directed and composed for by none other

---

[35] The letter, dated June 8, 1778, is found in *Papers*, 2:195–8. [Emphasis supplied.]

than the eminent *Kapellmeister,* Joseph Haydn. Did Jefferson intend to establish a small orchestra at Monticello and, perhaps, lead the ensemble with his violin? Leading with a violin was common at the time.[36]

It is intriguing to think that Jefferson might have done well as a conductor. Very probably he could read orchestral scores: his 1783 catalog of his personal library, which lists an extensive music collection, shows numerous orchestral works, suggesting that he was a sufficiently good violinist to have led an ensemble.[37] Including his wife Martha as ensemble player would have been inevitable. Her keyboard skills could have contributed greatly, since a harpsichordist was an eighteenth-century musical mainstay, supplying an essential part of the *basso continuo*—the bass line, harmony, and steady rhythm, all of which held an ensemble performance together. Mrs. Jefferson would probably have found such music-making a welcome relief from a life dominated by six pregnancies in an unfinished building filled with the din and the dust of perpetual cycles of construction.[38] Sadly, it appears that the letter to Signor Fabbroni was intercepted by the British and, therefore, never delivered to its intended recipient.[39] Fabbroni, alas, never sent any musician-servants to Monticello.

JEFFERSON'S ATTAINMENTS AS A VIOLINIST

Jefferson played the violin well, perhaps well enough to be called "outstanding" among his Virginia peers. For Jefferson, mastery of the violin was surely consistent with his basic drive towards excellence in all things. Every one of his interests became a challenge to his unbounded need to master everything: when he decided to build Monticello, he became an expert architect; when he chose the Roman style, he became an expert in Palladio's designs; when he needed heating sources for making bricks, he became an expert in stoves and brick-making; when he decided that Monticello's portico with Roman columns would best fulfill his aesthetic standards, he became an expert on Roman columns; when he decided to create a garden at Monticello, he became an expert botanist. It is patently clear that when Thomas

---

[36] For example, in a letter to his father from Paris dated July 3, 1778, Wolfgang Mozart refers to M. Lahoussaye, the first violinist, as the conductor of the concert spirituel orchestral: "I decided next morning not to go to the concert at all [premiering the *Paris* symphony at the concert spirituel]; but in the evening the weather being fine, I at last made up my mind to go, determined if my symphony went as badly as it did at the rehearsal I would certainly make my way into the orchestra, snatch the fiddle out of the hands of Lahoussaye, the first violin, and conduct myself!" Emily Anderson, *The Letters of Mozart and His Family Chronologically Arranged, Translated and Edited,* (London: Macmillan) 3rd edn., 1988, 557–558.

[37] A listing of Jefferson's entire 1783 music catalogue is contained in Appendix 2.

[38] Jack McLaughlin, *Jefferson and Monticello: The Biography of a Builder* (New York: Holt, 1988).

[39] *Papers,* 2:198.

Jefferson took up his violin he must have set the highest standards for himself as a performer on that instrument.

Testimonials to his violinistic skills came from friends as well as former enemies who were combatants against the revolutionary government of his new nation. In addition to the acceptance and praise of his playing prowess provided by friends such as Governor Fauquier and John Tyler, historians have uncovered even more objective evidence: the acclaim of British and Hessian military officers taken prisoner after the American victory at Saratoga in 1777, removed 700 miles or more from the battle zone, and quartered in and around Charlottesville.[40]

An eighteenth-century war among Europeans retained certain vestiges of chivalry, in that officers (almost always members of the aristocracy) who were captured in battle, while technically prisoners of war, were removed to areas behind the lines, "paroled," and allowed to participate in the social life of the local gentry. In Jefferson's world, gentlemen treated other gentlemen—no matter what their nationality or political persuasion—appropriately. Paroled Hessian and British officers were comfortably ensconced in plantations and rented homes near Monticello after Saratoga. Those who could play a musical instrument were often invited to Monticello for Jefferson's musical soirées.

Captain Bibby, an aide-de-camp to the British General Simon Fraser, is reported to have played violin duets with the Master of Monticello. Reputedly an excellent violinist, the Captain allegedly stated, in substance, that Mr. Jefferson was "the finest unprofessional [sic] player he ever heard on the instrument."[41]

Jacob Rubsamen, one of numerous Jefferson correspondents, sent a letter to Jefferson, dated December 1, 1780, while the latter was serving as Governor of Virginia. It contained the English translation of the text of a letter sent to Europe by an unnamed Hessian officer-prisoner—possibly Captain Baron von Geismar—on parole in the Charlottesville area. This letter was published in a Hamburg newspaper and its text copied and made part of another letter posted back to America to another Hessian officer-internee, Major-General Baron von Riedesel, who became a neighbor and even a family friend of Thomas and Martha Jefferson. It first describes their home at Monticello and closes with references to them in most admiring terms:

> *.... As all Virginians are fond of Music, he is particularly so. You will find in his House an*

---

[40] More than 4000 captured enemy officers and men were moved to the Charlottesville area. See *Memorandum & Account Books*, 1:477.

[41] H.S. Randall, *The Life of Thomas Jefferson*, 1:132–33, note 3.

FIGURE 4. *Imaginary rendition of a musical soirée at Monticello, with Jefferson performing on the violin along with a paroled enemy officer. (Rendition credited to Culver Pictures, Inc.)*

elegant Harpsichord Piano forte [sic] and some Violins. The latter he performs well upon himself, the former his Lady touches very skillfully and who, is in all Respects a very agreeable, Sensible, and Accomplished Lady.[42]

With his great gift for friendship, Jefferson formed many close and lasting relationships with a wide variety of people. Among these was another enemy captive, a Hessian officer, Captain Baron Friedrich von Geismar, also a violinist. The Baron had an elderly father in his homeland and very much wanted to be exchanged as a parolee for an American prisoner. The British, however, were not sufficiently responsive to his pleas. Jefferson intervened on the Baron's behalf and sought the assistance of Richard Henry Lee of the Virginia Delegation to the Continental Congress.[43] After a year and half, Jefferson received word that Baron von Geismar was in New York and finally on his way home. Before he left in November 1780, the Baron wrote a warm thank-you note to Jefferson, which ended with the following lines:

---

[42] *Papers*, 4:174. See also, Malone, 1:296. As Malone notes, the translation was presumably done by Rubsamen.

[43] *Papers*, 2:255.

.... Adieu. Be my friend, do not forget me and persuede [sic] Yourself of my Sincerity. My Respects to Mdm and the little Misses; Torriano [or "Dorriano"—a servant or friend?] has all my Musik for You.

—Geismar[44]

Jefferson admired von Geismar's playing and was very likely impressed with his collection of music for the violin. Von Geismar surely knew how much those musical scores meant to his friend and gave them to Jefferson as a token of gratitude for his help and as a salute to Jefferson's musical talent. A gift of music as a means of expressing gratitude for such an important favor attests to the significance of music to Jefferson.

In his 1858 biography, Henry S. Randall lavishly praised the Virginian's skill in playing the violin.[45] In contemporary written comments on that work, one of Patsy Jefferson Randolph's daughters, Ellen Wayles Randolph Coolidge, disagreed with Randall's assessment. She found the praise overstated and wrote:

With regard to Mr. Jefferson's skill on the violin I think that Mr. Libby's note says enough. Mr. Randall's idea that he became "one of the best violinists of his day" is a little extreme. My grandfather would I believe have disclaimed it. When we remember that the violin is a most difficult instrument, and that to attain great proficiency in the management of it requires the labour of a life—that sixteen hours out of the twenty-four have sometimes been devoted to it, we see at once that the time given to music by Mr. Jefferson could never have accomplished more than a gentlemanly proficiency. No amateur violinist could hope to equal a professor [sic]. Mr. Jefferson played I believe very well indeed, but not so well as to stand a comparison with many other persons especially such as he must have met with abroad....[46]

While it is accurate to say that Jefferson must have achieved less than complete professional mastery of the instrument, we must also observe that Ellen's judgment, based as it was on her personal experience with her grandfather's playing, was formed long past his prime as a violinist—and long after a severe injury to his right wrist (discussed below) greatly limited

---

[44] *Papers*, 4:173. In April, 1788, during the time when Jefferson was serving as American Minister to France, he met the Baron von Geismar in Frankfurt–am–Main on his way back to Paris after a diplomatic mission to the Netherlands. Jefferson spent four days with his old friend, and, as it was, made a final renewal of their most cordial relationship. See George Green Shackelford, *Thomas Jefferson's Travels in Europe, 1784–1789* (Baltimore: Johns Hopkins UP, 1995), 144–50.

[45] H.S. Randall, *The Life of Thomas Jefferson*, 1:131–132.

[46] Ellen Wayles Randolph Coolidge. Manuscript notebook, 36-37.

his bowing technique. Jefferson probably reached his peak as a violinist in 1782, fourteen years before his granddaughter was even born.

An American in Paris, 1784–1789

Monticello's domestic tranquillity was tragically interrupted by Martha Jefferson's untimely death in 1782. She died from the consequences of a difficult childbirth on her delicate constitution, a blow that sent Jefferson into prolonged and severe depression, one from which he never fully recovered. The two Marthas, his wife "Patty" and his daughter whom he called "Patsy," were the most important women in his life. There is, however, evidence of friendships with and attractions to some other women, including a brief Parisian romance with Maria Cosway (see below), as well as a strongly suspected liaison with Sally Hemings, a household slave.

Martha was gone, but Patsy, their oldest daughter, remained at her father's side for much of the rest of his life. It seemed like an act of Providence when Congress appointed him minister plenipotentiary to negotiate treaties of amity and commerce and sent him to France in the summer of 1784.[47] Jefferson took Patsy and slave James Hemings (whom he later freed) with him to Paris. When he arrived in Paris with Patsy in 1784, Jefferson immediately arranged for his daughter's admission to the city's finest educational institution, the Abbaye Royale de Panthémont, a convent school located in the Faubourg Saint-Germain.[48] Gaining her admission there was not easy, but thanks to the assistance of the Marquis de Chastellux it became a reality. Her father had ensured that she receive a thorough education with particular emphasis on music. The young lady took harpsichord lessons with Claude Balbastre, composer, organist at Notre Dame and St. Roche, and one of France's leading keyboard players. Patsy became an accomplished harpsichordist.

While Patsy was studying at the Abbaye Panthémont, Jefferson asked another friend, Dr. Charles Burney, the eminent English music historian, to supervise the construction of a new harpsichord for Patsy. Jacob Kirckman (also spelled "Kirkman"), a London craftsman, built

---

[47] The appointment was, in fact, just as likely a merciful act by his Virginia colleagues who wanted to rescue their friend from depression and, simultaneously, ensure that Virginia's proprietary interests were represented during the critical trade negotiations then occurring in France and affecting Virginia's economy. This was the third time Jefferson had been selected to represent his government in Paris. Appointed in July, 1781 by Congress as commissioner to help negotiate a peace treaty with the British, he declined the appointment for personal reasons, chiefly his wife's illness. Appointed again, in November, 1782, after Martha's death, he almost departed for France, but ice and British warships blockading the mouth of the Chesapeake prevented him from leaving. By April, 1783, the Treaty of Paris had been signed and his services as peace negotiator were no longer required. See W.S. Randall, *Jefferson: A Life*, 349–52.

[48] *Memorandum & Account Books*, 1:560-1, and especially n.84 therein.

the instrument according to Jefferson's exacting specifications. Two years later, in 1787, it was delivered to the ecstatic young lady in Paris. When Patsy returned to Virginia, her harpsichord was carefully packed and shipped to Monticello where it remained, beloved and well-played by its proud owner and others. Years later, Jefferson's granddaughters called it "Mama's old rattle-trap."[49]

Although the assignment to Paris marked a new era for the Master of Monticello, the shadows of his recent past, especially the loss of his beloved wife, were constantly with him. Another personal tragedy soon added to his sorrow. In January 1785, the marquis de Lafayette, a close friend, brought news that Jefferson's daughter Lucy Elizabeth, barely two years old, had died from the complications of whooping cough. "Nabby" (later sometimes known as "Abigail II") Adams, daughter of Abigail and John Adams, noted in her diary that Jefferson was in "a confirmed state of melancholy" and withdrew from society and friends for a while.[50]

While grief surely curtailed his social engagements, it did not seem to lessen his considerable achievements in international diplomacy. Congress had already sent Benjamin Franklin and John Adams to Paris as Commissioners for treaty negotiations. However, Dr. Franklin, in his 79th year, was not well and wished to retire. Thomas Jefferson's arrival relieved the tension between the homespun, easygoing Dr. Franklin and the sometimes-prickly John Adams. In negotiating a commercial treaty with Prussia, Jefferson espoused the more humane treatment of prisoners of war. Anticipating European cynicism, he authored a paper promoting the humane treatment of prisoners of war, entitled "Reasons in Support of the New Proposed Articles in the Treaties of Commerce." This treatise, well-received by the Prussians, expressed a respect for human dignity and human rights, which later became a pillar of American political philosophy. It has been quoted often by American presidents throughout the nation's history.

Before anyone else noticed, Jefferson sensed French designs on colonizing parts of the New World, specifically the Pacific Northwest. After he informed Admiral John Paul Jones, he corresponded with the American Foreign Affairs Secretary, John Jay, who followed the situation closely. The French effort to explore and possibly to colonize this area was abandoned. In the company of Adams, he later renegotiated Dutch loans to the United States, a tremendous accomplishment because Amsterdam bankers needed quick repayment due to political and economic turmoil in the Netherlands. He helped negotiate new trade agreements with

---

[49] Cripe, 1.

[50] William Howard Adams, *The Paris Years of Thomas Jefferson* (New Haven, [Conn.]: Yale UP, 1997), 181.

France for tobacco and the whale oil used to light the street lamps of Paris. Because Jefferson kept busy, he was soon able to shed his grief and to harvest some of the cultural abundance around him.

What an extraordinary experience Europe must have been for this keen-thinking, consummately curious Virginian who found himself in the company of some of the giants of the French enlightenment! How extraordinary for him to meet and converse with Europe's greatest musicians, artists, scientists, philosophers and statesmen! Thomas Jefferson, who jokingly referred to himself in correspondence as a "savage of the mountains of America,"[51] but with the title of American Minister Plenipotentiary to France, was able to breathe the rarified air found at the height of late eighteenth-century Parisian culture while performing extraordinary diplomatic service on behalf of his country.

His vigorous social life in Paris encompassed theaters, concerts and intellectual soirées. Lafayette quickly brought him into his inner circle of literati and *philosophes*, all gentlemen like Jefferson—and most with similar democratic views. Prominent among them were Louis Alexandre, the duc de La Rochefoucauld; the marquis de Condorcet, the famous mathematician; the marquis de Chastellux, who had visited Jefferson at Monticello in April, 1782; Jean-François Marmontel, the famed playwright and librettist who wrote the *libretti* of many an opera Jefferson attended in Paris; the abbé Morellet, a renowned *philosophe;* and the baron Friedrich Melchior de Grimm, minister of Saxe-Gotha and an avid literary critic of whom Jefferson was especially fond. The group's conversations ranged from politics and science to literature, poetry, theater, and, of course, music.

Jefferson would likely have recalled the earlier soirées in Williamsburg when he was a guest of Governor Fauquier. He must have felt at home in Paris with this illustrious group. He had read Rabelais and Montesquieu in the original French while a student and appears to have handled the language adequately. William H. Adams observes that Jefferson expressed himself in "'resounding abstractions' and bold, sweeping generalizations very much in the contemporary French rhetorical style."[52] Jefferson's manner had a suavity, excitement and open-mindedness that made him attractive to French society, where discussions of literature, fine arts, music, and other learned subjects flourished.[53] Paris was at

---

[51] Thomas Jefferson to Charles Bellini, 30 Sep 1785, Jefferson, *Papers*, 8:568-70. Bellini was professor of modern languages at the College of William and Mary.

[52] Adams, *Paris Years*, 184.

[53] The musical atmosphere there invites comparison with the Court of Frederick the Great in Potsdam in the late 1740s, when Johann Sebastian Bach was a guest of the flute-playing Prussian king at Sans-Souci. Paris was in many ways the intellectual capital of the world, although the French Revolution was soon to change all that.

FIGURE 5. *Portrait of Thomas Jefferson painted in Paris, 1788 by Jefferson's good friend, John Trumbull, at the request of Maria Cosway. The canvas was taken to Lodi, Italy, by Mrs. Cosway and remained there for almost two hundred years. It was given to the people of the United States by the Italian government in 1976. (White House Historical Association)*

that moment the western world's center of cultural activity, and Jefferson gleaned as much from it as he could.

He probably learned from Dr. Franklin that most cultural and political activities in Paris took place in the salons of famous hostesses. These were charming, witty, excellent conversationalists—aristocrats, usually of great wealth—well-versed in literature, the fine arts and music, and were, in some cases, authors themselves. In their salons they introduced Europe's most famous performing artists to Parisian society. Jefferson was in frequent attendance. He was a favorite of the famous Madame de Staël, Madame d'Houdetot, and the duchesse d'Anville. Jefferson was especially close to the comtesse de Tessé, Lafayette's aunt, a talented painter and horticulturist. Years later President Jefferson wrote to her: "The friendship with which you honored me in Paris was among the circumstances which most contributed to my happiness there."[54]

At abbé Morellet's matinées, the Virginian discussed politics with the duc de La Rochefoucauld and mathematics with the marquis de Condorcet. The duchesse d'Abrantés noted that abbé Morellet's salon overlooked the Tuileries Gardens "amidst perfect quiet and with peace in one's heart and soul one listened to the most ravishing music, or to discussions of the latest poetry and prose."[55] Many of the *grandes dames* who befriended the tall widower from America were arbiters of French culture.

Several of Jefferson's American women friends visited him while he was in Paris. Anne

---

[54] Andrew Burstein, *The Inner Jefferson: Portrait of a Grieving Optimist* (Charlottesville: UP of Virginia, 1995), 73. See letter to Mdm Tessé 30 Jan 1803, Library of Congress.

[55] Marie Goebel Kimball, *Jefferson: the Scene of Europe 1784 to 1789* (New York: Coward-McCann, 1950), 97.

Willing Bingham, the stunning wife of a wealthy Philadelphia businessman who was in Paris for commercial reasons, was one. Another was Angelica Schuyler Church, who came from a prominent upstate New York family. She was the sister-in-law of Alexander Hamilton. Jefferson wrote thoughtful letters to Angelica, sometimes with a touch of flirtation. He held her in high esteem.

First, however, among American women to provide attentive caring to Mr. Jefferson in France was Abigail Adams. The two quickly became friends and then corresponded for decades thereafter. Jefferson instantly grasped that this remarkable, intelligent, mostly self-educated lady with high moral standards and integrity was no less admirable than the *grandes dames* of the Parisian salons. Their extensive correspondence touched on each other's interests, which included literature, the arts, and politics.

Mrs. Adams demonstrated genuine sensitivity to the cultural experiences which pleased Jefferson the most: in her first letter to Jefferson after she left Paris for London in late May, 1785 (where Mr. Adams had been appointed ambassador to the Court of St. James), she wrote, after a performance in Westminster Abbey,

> *I went last week to hear the Musick in Westminster Abbey. [Handel's] Messiah was perfor-md. It was Sublime beyond description. I most sincerely wisht for your presence as **your favorite passion** would have received the highest gratification. I should have sometimes fancied myself amongst a higher order of Beings: if it had not been for a very troublesome female, who was unfortunately seated behind me: and whose volubility not all the powers of Musick could still...*[56]

Andrew Burstein also notes that Mrs. Adams appreciated Jefferson's reciprocal sensitivity in understanding the complicated emotional makeup of her husband.[57] Jefferson admired Mrs. Adams even during the very difficult political circumstances surrounding the 1800 presidential campaign, in which he was pitted against her husband. Again, the Virginian's talent for friendship brought forth a lasting relationship.

Jefferson's whirlwind romance with Maria Cosway in Paris, August to October 1786, was one of the happiest times of his life. Mrs. Cosway, the vivacious and beautiful wife of a successful English portrait painter, Richard Cosway,[58] was herself a gifted painter, composer,

---

[56] Richard Alan Ryerson, ed., et al., *Adams Family Correspondence* (Cambridge: Belknap, 1993), 171. [Emphasis supplied]

[57] Burstein, 8.

[58] For an enlightening discussion of Jefferson and the Cosways, see Shackelford, 65–74, "Richard and Maria's

harpist and organist who sang while accompanying herself on the piano (or on the harp) with music of her own composition.

Although she was of English parentage, she had grown up in Italy. Together for six weeks, Jefferson and Maria were inseparable. Together they attended the Paris Opéra, the salon matinées, and a number of concerts. They visited the harpist-composer Johann Baptiste Krumpholtz. Maria even composed a cycle of songs in Italian dedicated to her Virginia admirer. After she returned to London with her husband, she and Jefferson carried on a desultory written correspondence. Maria later returned to Paris while Jefferson was still there, but the joy of their first time together was not renewed in any meaningful way. They wrote to each other occasionally for several

Fig. 6. Maria Cosway, a self-portrait. Mezzotint by Valentine Green, 1787. (Collection of William S. Adams)

decades, but the guardedly intimate relationship they first formed in Paris did not continue.[59]

Without doubt, the time Jefferson spent in Paris nurtured his love of music. Musical activity was intense—and he reveled in it. In a 1785 letter from Paris to Charles Bellini (then an émigré living in Virginia), Jefferson uncharacteristically exposed the intensity of his feelings about the musical experiences he was then having in Paris:

> *Were I to proceed to tell you how much I enjoy their architecture, sculpture, painting, music I should want words. It is in these arts they [i.e., the French] shine. The last of them, particularly, is an enjoyment, the deprivation of which with us, cannot be calculated. I am almost ready to say, it is the only thing which from my heart I envy them, and which, in spite of all the authority of the Decalogue, I do covet.*[60]

---

marriage was not exactly an arranged one, but it is clear that it was one of convenience. Richard seems to have been more complaisant about Maria's admirers than he was accepting of her artistic career."

[59] Another and equally fascinating discussion of Jefferson's experiences with Maria Cosway is contained in Adams, 222–50.

[60] Thomas Jefferson to Charles Bellini, Jefferson, *Writings*, 834.

Besides opera, Paris's most illustrious musical events were the orchestral performances called *le concert spirituel* ("sacred concert"). Founded in 1725, the concert spirituel initially performed only sacred music during Lent, while the opera was closed. By Jefferson's day, however, secular music had long supplanted the sacred, and the concert spirituel presented all types of concert music. About thirty concerts per year were given in the Salle des Machines of the Chateau des Tuileries and featured recently composed works by the best soloists, with an orchestra and voices drawn from the Paris Opéra.[61] Until the French Revolution it offered one of the largest and best orchestras in Europe, surpassed only by the Mannheim orchestra, which Mozart admired so much.

Joseph Haydn, Johann Christian Bach, and Mozart—all wrote compositions for the concert spirituel. Monsieur Legros, the music director and later a Jefferson friend, commissioned a symphony from the 22-year-old Wolfgang Mozart in 1778 for a June concert. The work became an instant hit, being performed at two successive concerts spirituel. The work later became known as the composer's "Paris" Symphony.[62]

Jefferson's meticulously-maintained account books attest that he frequently attended M. Legros' concerts. In fact, they show that he was an enthusiastic concert- and opera-goer the entire time he was abroad. Appendix 4 is a tabulation of the entries related to ticket purchases for musical events shown by his account books while he was American Minister to France. In summary, between September 8, 1784 and May 27, 1789, they show that he bought tickets, usually at a price of six French francs, to no less than fifteen concerts spirituel and five benefit concerts, most held at the Panthéon (a different building than the current Parisian Panthéon) and in the Salle des Machines, three of these latter four concerts given by and for the benefit of performing violinists. Jefferson also attended at least one concert in London while visiting American ambassador John Adams and, several years later, one at Amsterdam while on a diplomatic mission. Also, during the period September 2, 1784 to January 14, 1786, he bought tickets for three works given at the Paris Opéra and for eleven additional evenings of opera (often performances of two or even three works of somewhat lighter musical fare than the sort given at the Opéra) given at the Comédie-Italienne, a venue occupying the site of the present Opéra Comique on the Boulevard des Italiens. While visiting his diplomatic colleague, John Adams, he also apparently bought a seat for Salieri's *opera buffa*, *La*

---

[61] For a comprehensive study of the concert spirituel, see Constant Pierre, *Histoire du Concert Spirituel 1725-1790* (Paris: Heugel et Cie, 1975). See also discussion of *le concert spirituel* in *Memorandum & Account Books*, 1:562, n. 93.

[62] The composition, also known as Mozart's Symphony No. 31, is in D Major, Köchel Verzeichnis (KV) number 297. See also, Pierre, *Histoire du Concert Spirituel,* 309.

Scuola de' Gelosi, at the King's Theatre, Haymarket, London, at a royal command performance before the Prince of Wales.[63]

But these ticket purchases alone, impressive though they may be when considering Jefferson's frequent and extensive travels and sometimes burdensome social and diplomatic responsibilities,[64] surely understate his intense participation in Parisian—indeed, European— musical life. It is beyond question that he was frequently a guest of highly-placed friends at many of the concerts, operas, recitals, and soirées that were constantly taking place in the French capital. He had no need to purchase tickets for those events, so he, of course, did not record them as expenses. As James A. Bear and Lucia C. Stanton point out in a footnote to their astonishingly well-annotated and helpful two-volume opus on which Appendix 4 is based, *Jefferson's Memorandum Books: Accounts, with Legal Records and Miscellany, 1767-1826*, "The extent of [Jefferson's] attendance at the Opera and other spectacles cannot be gauged from [Account Book] entries alone; many of his friends, among them Madame de Corny, the Comtesse d'Houdetot, Chastellux and Chalut de Verin, had permanent boxes at the Opera and customarily treated their dinner guests to a night at the theatre."[65]

It is worth examining for a moment the programs of the concert and opera performances for which Jefferson purchased tickets.[66] By today's standards, these performances— whether given in the Salle des Machines, at the Panthéon, at the Opéra, or at the Comédie-Italienne—were amazingly lengthy. Two symphonies, very often composed by Joseph

---

[63] Shackelford, 47. Shackelford notes that "While he was in London, Jefferson attended the theatre and opera three or four times at Covent Garden, Drury Lane, and the Haymarket." See also, *Memorandum & Account Books*, 1:614, n. 51.

[64] Jefferson was often obliged to leave Paris on short trips, not only to Versailles but also Fontainebleau, where the French Court relocated in early autumn to accommodate the king's desire to hunt hares. Jefferson also traveled to visit John Adams in England for about two months, from March 6, to May 1, 1786. In an unofficial capacity, Jefferson left Paris on February 28, 1787 and journeyed to the south of France, spent about three weeks in Northern Italy and returned to the French capital via the Languedoc, Gascony, Toulouse, Bordeaux, Brittany and the Loire Valley, finally arriving in Paris on June 10-a trip of more than three months. Jefferson's last major European excursion was to the Netherlands to attempt to shore up shaky American credit with nervous Dutch bankers. (He, in the company of John Adams, was successful in doing so.) The journey began from Paris on March 4, 1788, but, after concluding the financial business at hand in Amsterdam, Jefferson took a decidedly circuitous route home via Utrecht through the Rhineland (in part to see his friend von Geismar and the Rhine grape-growing regions) then to Strasbourg, and returned to Paris on April 23, some fifty-three days after having left. These three visits alone consumed some 200 days. See Shackelford, 31-42; 43-63; 75-127; 129-156.

[65] *Memorandum & Account Books*, 1:582. The editors' authority for this proposition is Ernest Boyesse, *Les Abonnés de l'Opéra 1783-1786* (Paris: 1881).

[66] We have an idea of their programs because most concerts and operas were listed in advertisements or notices published in the daily Parisian newspaper of the era, the *Journal de Paris*.

Haydn,[67] interspersed with several vocal pieces, a concerto, a pianoforte (or other instrumental) sonata, and a duet (or even two) were *de rigueur*. The concert spirituel for June 15, 1786, for which Jefferson paid six francs, is fairly representative: two symphonies by Haydn; airs by Sarti and J.G. Naumann; a *symphonie concertante* by Davaux; an oratorio, *Esther*, by Sacchini, the opera composer (and rival of Piccinni's [see below]); and, finally, works by La Manière, J.G. Burhoefer, and L.C. Ragué played by the prodigy-harpists, the sisters Descarsins, ages seven and twelve.[68] With the exception of Haydn, few German or Austrian composers were favored; most were French or Italian. It appears, however, that Jefferson did hear at least one work by Wolfgang Mozart, a piano concerto (which one isn't indicated), on December 26, 1785.[69]

To obtain access to the then-burgeoning world of European opera, the tickets Jefferson bought were for, more often as not, French comic works, particularly light comic pieces, such as *Silvain*, *Aucassin et Nicollete*, *Zemire et Azor*, and *La Fausse Magie*, each of the four composed by the acclaimed André Grétry,[70] with a libretto by Jefferson's Parisian friend, Jean-François Marmontel. Jefferson also seems to have favored Italian operatic works, particularly those by Niccolò Piccinni:[71]

> *T[homas] J[efferson] apparently never recorded his opinion of the still smoldering controversy between the partisans of Gluck and Piccinni, but he clearly favored the Italian style of*

---

[67] Joseph Haydn's music was immensely popular in Paris at this time. In fact, at the concert spirituel between the years 1777 and 1790 his works were performed 256 times, far more than any other non-French composer. Pierre, *Histoire du Concert Spirituel,* 175. In 1784-5, a concert enterprise related to a Masonic lodge, Le Loge Olympique, offered Haydn a handsome remuneration for six new symphonies, now known as the composer's "Paris" symphonies, numbers 82-87, and written during 1785-86. "The six works, nos. 82-87, became very popular in Paris...." H. C. Robbins Landon and David Wyn Jones, *Haydn: His Life and Music* (Bloomington: Indiana UP, 1988), 175. Along with their characteristically imaginative orchestration, particularly in the strings, Haydn's *Paris* symphonies "stand out for their marked personality, comparable only to the expressive symphonies of about 1770 and the London symphonies of 1791-5." Jens Peter Larsen, "Haydn, (Franz) Joseph," *New Grove Dictionary*, 8:740.

[68] *Memorandum & Account Books*, 1:630

[69] *Memorandum & Account Books*, 1:604

[70] André-Ernest-Modest Grétry (1741-1813) held the supreme position among composers of French comic operas in the latter part of the eighteenth century. He was trained in Liège and Rome and became an overnight sensation when, in 1768, his comic opera *Le huron* (with libretto by Marmontel) was produced in Paris. Grétry's music exhibits Italian influences in melodic line and declamatory style, which he transformed through an innate sense of proportion and highly refined taste into charming expressions of humor, elegance and subtlety.

[71] Niccolò Piccinni (1728-1800), a pillar of late eighteenth-century Italian and French opera, received his early musical training in Naples. Later moving to Rome where he demonstrated his amazing talent for turning out opera after opera (at least 100) for production in Rome, Naples and other major Italian cities, he became the stuff of local legend. Dr. Burney met him in 1770 and referred to Piccinni as "a lively agreeable little man, rather grave for an Italian so full of fire and genius." After a falling-out with the fickle Roman public, Piccinni traveled

the latter. Two of his three recorded visits to the Paris Opera were to hear Piccinni works. Jean François Marmontel, the leading Piccinnist and librettist of Didon, was a regular guest at [Jefferson's] table, and [Jefferson] consulted Piccinni on the merits of the piano.[72]

Not long after John and Abigail Adams and their family arrived in Paris in August, 1784, Mr. Jefferson took their children to a concert spirituel.[73] The *Memorandum and Account Books* show that Jefferson bought tickets for only one concert spirituel during the fall of 1784, and that there were only two concerts spirituels given during that period, i.e., on October 4 and November 1. The diary of the "younger Abigail" (i.e., "Nabby") establishes that she and her brother, John Quincy, attended the October 4 concert along with Mr. Jefferson.[74]

In December, 1785, Jefferson almost certainly heard the celebrated Mlle. Rose Renaud sing at two concert spirituels for which he had purchased tickets, because, in a letter dated December 27, 1785, to Abigail Adams he stated that "Mademoiselle Renaud, of 16. years of age sings as nobody ever sung before."[75]

Jefferson was not hesitant to be critical of singers when the occasion warranted it. He had been in the audience at the Comédie-Italienne in June, 1786, when Madame Dugazon, with great success, had appeared as Nina in Dalayrac's comic opera *Nina ou la folle par amour*. Months later, in March, 1787, while visiting Aix in Provence, he wrote his devoted secretary, William Short, in Paris that he had attended performances of *Alexis and Justine* and *Mazet*, where the prima donna, a young woman from Marseilles, had impressed him in being "clear [unlike Mdme Dugazon and the "other celebrated ones of Paris"] of that dreadful wheeze or rather whistle in respiration which resembles the agonizing struggles for breath of a dying person."[76]

There can be little doubt that the detailed expense records in Jefferson's own hand which have fortunately come down to us[77] provide solid evidence that western art music was quite

to Paris in 1776, where he and a group of believers immediately went into competition with Gluck and his followers. He composed and helped produce both *opere buffe* and *opere serie* in Paris for more than ten years and achieved no small measure of success in melding a traditional Italian dramatic and lyrical approach to opera with a more contemporary French operatic style.

[72] *Memorandum & Account Books*, 1:597, n. 96.

[73] Kimball, *Jefferson: The Scene of Europe, 1784 to 1789*, 244.

[74] *Memorandum & Account Books*, 1:566.

[75] Thomas Jefferson to Abigail Adams, 27 Dec 1785; *Papers*, 9:126

[76] Thomas Jefferson to William Short, 29 Mar 1787, *Papers*, 11:254–55.

[77] The original eleven bound volumes of Jefferson's Memorandum and Account Books are in five different repositories: the Library of Congress, Washington, D.C.; the Massachusetts Historical Society, Boston; University of Virginia, Charlottesville; the Henry E. Huntington Library, San Marino, California; the New York Public Library, New York, NY.

a bit more than mere entertainment for this man: it was food for his inquiring mind and, truly, as he had written to Giovanni Fabbroni in the previous decade, "the favorite passion of [his] soul."

In 1785 Paris was also a violin player's Mecca. Jefferson certainly must have heard many famous touring artists while he was a Parisian resident. We know from his bookkeeping that he obtained tickets to the benefit concert for the so-called mulatto child-prodigy violinist, George Bridgetower.[78] He also attended performances, presumably at Versailles, by the eighteenth century's premier violinist, Giovanni Battista Viotti.[79]

Viotti was to eighteenth-century violin playing what Paganini represented to the nineteenth century.[80] He was student of Pugnani's and came from the Italian violin school, but Paris was his real home. Viotti's debut at a concert spirituel in 1782 was an unparalleled sensation. He was an imposing figure on stage with his Stradivari violin and, quite possibly, new Tourte bow. He drew sonorities from his instrument that sophisticated Parisian audiences had never before heard. His tone was a large and beautiful *cantabile*. He employed oscillating passagework with multiple stops, chords, novel bowing-strokes, and special effects such as the use of the G-string's high register, an area neglected until Viotti. Viotti's expressive style with dynamic nuances and a sense of drama were his outstanding attributes, and his technical contributions were far ahead of his time. Some of his twenty-nine violin *concerti* are still in the modern violinist's repertoire. Concerto No. 22 in A minor, as performed by Joachim in 1878, drew enthusiastic comments from Brahms in correspondence with Clara Schumann.[81]

Viotti has been called the "founder of the 'modern' (19th century) French school of violin-playing."[82] Even though after only a few years of giving public concerts he (temporarily) renounced public performance and entered Marie Antoinette's service with the seemingly lowly title of *accompagnateur*, his influence was enormous and pervasive. His concerts continued, on his terms, at Versailles. He attracted such disciples as Pierre Marie Baillot, Pierre Anton Rode, and Rodolphe Kreutzer.[83] Since the violin was so close to

---

[78] The concert was on May 27, 1789, at the Panthéon, and is Jefferson's last entry for concert tickets in Paris. The French Revolution was about to break out in earnest. *Memorandum & Account Books*, 1:734.

[79] Jefferson stated to Nicholas Trist in 1826 that "I have heard Viotti often." Jefferson allegedly added, however, that he "never derived the same pleasure from him that I have from Alberti." H.S. Randall, *The Life of Thomas Jefferson*, 1:131. See n. 30 and accompanying text for details about Francis Alberti.

[80] Franz Farga, *Violins and Violinists*, trans. E. Larsen, (New York: Praeger, 1940), 150–54.

[81] See Chappell White, "Viotti," *New Grove Dictionary*, 19: 864–66.

[82] Same, 864.

[83] Kreutzer played with Beethoven in Vienna and was the recipient of the dedication to Beethoven's Sonata in A Major, Opus 47, for violin and piano, the "Kreutzer" sonata. He authored an important violin method, still a guide for contemporary violinists.

his heart, Jefferson also made it a point to hear Paul Alday, one of Viotti's better-known students, and another Viotti pupil, Madame Gautherot, at the Musée de Paris on the Rue Dauphine.[84]

A "RIGHT HAND... DISABLED"

It is ironic that not long after after Jefferson, the violinist, reached the zenith of his musical development, his ability to play was devastated by a crippling compound fracture of his right wrist.[85] At the very same time (September, 1786), he also suffered a great emotional wound: Jefferson learned that Maria Cosway was soon to leave Paris. Maria's husband, Richard, had decided that they should return to London, and she was compelled to comply with his wishes. Jefferson was losing the object of his affections, and perhaps provoked by emotional turmoil, then suffered a physical injury that permanently circumscribed his future performance on the violin. According to one story, Jefferson rushed to Maria for a last meeting and, in a failed leap over a fountain while in a state of euphoria, fell to the pavement and shattered his right wrist. Another story involves a fall after his attempted vault over a fence before helping Maria over it.[86] A later account is found in a letter to President Jefferson from William Goldsmith, a Paris-based bookseller: ".... [W]hen your Excellency had the misfortune to hurt his Arm by a fall from his horse, while living at Challiot the writer was honored to write dictated by your Excellency himself."[87]

Can these three different explanations be reconciled? Probably not, but one thing is clear: Jefferson more or less permanently disabled his right wrist in some incident that he considered a "folly." In a subsequent letter to his friend Colonel Smith, Jefferson characteristically kept exactly what happened to him a private matter, "How the right hand became disabled would be a long story for the left to tell. It was by one of those follies from which good cannot come, but ill may."[88]

According to Jefferson's justly famous letter to Maria Cosway on October 12, 1786, often called "Dialogue Between My Head and My Heart,"[89] a surgeon had been called to help heal

---

[84] *Memorandum & Account Books*, I:604–5, n. 16 & 609, n. 33.

[85] L.H. Butterfield, and Howard C. Rice, Jr., "Jefferson's Earliest Note to Maria Cosway With Some New Facts and Conjectures on His Broken Wrist," *William and Mary Quarterly*, Jan., 1948, vol. 5, no. 1:26–33. See also, *Memorandum & Account Books*, 1:639, n.65 for an excellent discussion of the facts and consequences of this accident.

[86] W.S. Randall, *Jefferson: A Life*, 443–44.

[87] Letter, William Goldsmith to Thomas Jefferson, 20 Apr., 1807. Letter in Library of Congress.

[88] Thomas Jefferson to William Smith, 12 Oct. 1786, *Papers*, 10:478.

[89] Thomas Jefferson to Maria Cosway, 12 Oct. 1786. *Papers*, 10:443–453 and n. 79b, p. 453.

the injury which had occurred on or about September 18,[90] but no Parisian doctor Jefferson consulted seemed able to set the wrist correctly.

On February 11, 1787, nearly five months after the injury, Jefferson wrote Count Charles Gravier de Vergennes, the French Foreign Minister: "My hand is recovering very slowly from the effects of it's [sic] dislocation, I am advised by the Surgeons to try the waters of Aix en Provence."[91] Jefferson made the trip and arrived in Aix on March 25, 1787. The thermal treatments he received—some forty *douches* of 90° F. water over four days—were "without any sensible benefit" to his wrist.[92]

Although the acute pain eventually subsided, it is quite probable that he suffered significant discomfort from this injury for the rest of his life. He had a much-restricted range of motion that almost certainly attenuated performance on his beloved instrument.

Jefferson's wrist injury has apparently not previously been analyzed in a published writing by a knowledgeable musician/physician. The following analysis was graciously contributed by a trained violinist and board-certified doctor of internal medicine, Robert E. Belknap, M.D., of Mill Valley, California:

> *If we assume that Thomas Jefferson fell forward after a failed jump or a fall from a horse, and that his ensuing wrist fracture continued to cause pain long after his accident, then we might reasonably conclude that the fracture line involved the right wrist joint surface. A fracture into the joint surface tends to stay painful, while a fracture of the lower forearm or wrist above the joint tends to become pain-free. We have Jefferson's statements that the bones at the site of the injury were improperly set and were deformed, stiff, and painful for many years following the event. Given these assumptions and statements, how might an intra-articular wrist fracture affect his bowing technique?*
>
> *Assuming he suffered the most common type of injury, i.e., from a fall forward onto the outstretched hand, fractures of the radius (one of the two bones of the forearm; the other is the ulna) would result in at least two diminished motions at the right wrist: Jefferson would have experienced reduced ulnar deviation (less sideways motion toward the fifth finger), and reduced dorsiflexion (extension upward at the wrist with bow in hand). The reader may approximate this disability by splinting the wrist with a tightly wound towel and safety pin, then observe the limited motion at the wrist. Because of reduced ulnar deviation,*

---

[90] *Memorandum & Account Books*, 1:639, n.65

[91] Thomas Jefferson to Vergennes, 11 Feb 1787, *Papers* 11:140.

[92] Ray and Alma Moore, *Thomas Jefferson's Journey to the South of France* (New York: Stewart, Tabori & Chang, 1999),13. See also, Thomas Jefferson to William Short, 7 Apr 1787, *Papers* 11:280.

the travel of Jefferson's bow would have been abridged, permitting effective contact from the tip to about halfway down the bow, rather than over its full length. Also, smooth transition over the strings, from the G to the E, would have been impaired, as some wrist flexion/ dorsiflexion is required for this maneuver—even with active vertical arm motion at the shoulder. Mr. Jefferson would no longer enjoy sounding an arpeggio. In summary, his painful wrist with its impaired motion would reduce effective bow travel and impede smooth crossing of the strings. These are significant consequences for the serious violinist.[93]

The critical importance of flexibility in a string player's bow arm has been recently restated by none other than the renowned American violin virtuoso, Isaac Stern, who, in his 1999 autobiography, *My First 79 Years*, remarks:

The bow arm is, after all, the voice box, the throat, the tongue, the speaking individuality of every performer. Bow control, bow speed, and vibrato are three of the elements that differentiate one player from everyone else. The greater the flexibility, the greater the range of emotion and thought that can be expressed.[94]

In his book, Mr. Stern describes in detail how in 1957 a sprain of his right wrist brought on by an energetic tennis game kept him from playing the violin for three weeks—even after expert orthopedic care, which included complete wrist immobilization.[95] It takes little effort, then, to understand the catastrophic effect of Jefferson's improperly set right wrist *compound fracture* on his violin playing.

When Jefferson wrote the "Dialogue" letter to Maria Cosway, the pain and swelling in his right wrist forced him to write with his left hand.[96] The beginning of that correspondence provides a rare peek at the emotional state of this most private of individuals:

[My Dear] Madam: Paris, Octob. 12. 1786
Having performed the last sad office of handing you into your carriage at the Pavillon de St. Denis, and seen the wheels get actually into motion, I turned on my heel & walked, more dead than alive, to the opposite door, where my own was awaiting me.[97]

---

[93] Personal communication with the writer, 10 Aug. 1999.

[94] Issac Stern, with Chaim Potok, *My First 79 Years* (Knopf: New York, 1999), 306.

[95] Same, 135-138.

[96] See Appendix 5 for a facsimile of the page of Jefferson's account books that shows just how his handwriting changed after his injury and for other interesting entries, such as tickets to a concert spirituel and to an opera that he undoubtedly attended with Mrs. Cosway.

[97] *Papers*, 10:443.

Until Maria's departure, Jefferson was—to use a French (as well as an English) descriptive—*exuberant* in Paris. He was serving his country's interests well, he was in love with the musical, intellectual, and artistic riches that the French capital offered, and he was in love with an exciting and beautiful woman who shared these riches with him. When the carriage door closed behind Maria, he must have realized that the door also shut on a most happy period of his life. He had been wounded in heart and body. What was left for this desolate man?

In the past, playing his violin had eased the pain of losing a loved one, but now his crippled playing hand and wrist could not assist in delivering relief for his latest loss. Jefferson must have wondered if he would ever again play the violin with skill. He may have hoped to try performing again, since he purchased what he noted was a "small violin" in Paris[98] in the summer of 1788 and purchased "violin strings" (for $2.06) as late as 1793, in Philadelphia.[99] Other than these few factual tidbits, however, there is no other proof that he regularly played the violin from the time of his wrist injury until after he retired from his second term as President of the United States in 1809. We believe from family accounts, however, that in retirement the Master of Monticello often played the violin for his grandchildren on wintry afternoons.

JEFFERSON AND MUSIC AFTER PARIS

Jefferson's golden Parisian sojourn came to an end in September 1789. He had witnessed many (and even discreetly participated in a few) of the opening political struggles of the French Revolution, but, in August—and with two years yet to run on his appointment as Minister to France—he received permission to return to America on a few months' leave of absence. He sailed to Norfolk, Virginia in October. After five years abroad, he felt a strong urge to attend to personal affairs in Virginia and an even stronger urge to return his daughters to their native land. Dumas Malone in *Jefferson and the Rights of Man*, the second volume of his monumental biographical study, muses about some of the images that must have passed through Jefferson's mind on his voyage back home:

> *[Jefferson's experiences in France were] [a] bright chapter [in the story of his expanding thoughts and hopes] despite the dark background of European despotism, and he must have thought it also an extraordinarily rich one. Perhaps not even he could completely catalogue*

---

[98] This could well have been a *pochette* or "kit" instrument; the purchase price was 36 livres. *Memorandum & Account Books*, Aug. 15, 1788, 1:712.

[99] *Memorandum & Account Books*, 1:907.

his observations and acquisitions in the realms of art and architecture, agriculture and household furniture, science and invention. But he could think of the books and plants and drawings he had sent or was sending home, of the furnishings he had left in [his Parisian residence] the Hôtel de Langeac, of the pictures he had bought or ordered, of the wines he was shipping, of the vineyards and rice fields he had observed in Burgundy and Bordeaux and Lombardy. Many of these things he could take with him. They could go in boxes or be preserved in letters and memoranda. They were his to give or keep for the rest of life. He could even put musical scores in boxes, as actually he did; but until he returned to Europe, such concerts as he had heard in Paris could be only be a memory—less real than pictures of the Maison Carrée or the Hôtel de Salm. Only in Europe could the favorite passion of his soul be fully satisfied. More even than Maria Cosway, the music which had delighted him must have seemed like a lovely dream as he listened to the lapping of the waves.[100]

Jefferson seems to have planned to return to France the following spring. That was not to be.

Even before he left Europe, Jefferson let it be known that he was disinterested in high public office at home: once his European assignment was concluded, he yearned to spend the rest of his life in "domestic tranquillity" at his beloved Monticello, still only partially completed yet already in serious disrepair. But George Washington had other plans for Mr. Jefferson: he wanted him as his Secretary of State, and, because he had the most profound respect for the new President, Jefferson concluded he could not refuse; after two months' delay, he accepted the appointment. In 1790, after Patsy's wedding to Thomas Mann Randolph, Jr. at Monticello, the nation's new Secretary of State left for New York, the temporary national capital, travelling through Philadelphia, where he paid a last visit to his old friend, Benjamin Franklin.

As Secretary of State, Jefferson moved with the government to Philadelphia in the fall of 1790. He enjoyed the rich musical offerings of Philadelphia and must have learned from the many talented musicians who wrote, performed and taught there. The prime mover in Philadelphia's musical circles was Alexander Reinagle, conductor, composer and director of a music theater company. John Christopher Moller was also important in Philadelphia as a composer, publisher, organist and harpsichordist. Since Moller was a friend of Jefferson's and had given harpsichord lessons to Jefferson's younger daughter, Polly, years before, it seems highly likely that he and Jefferson together discussed music. Henry Capron was another

---

[100] Malone, vol. 2, *Jefferson and the Rights of Man*, 242–243.

Philadelphian musically active at the same time. Jefferson probably heard him play the cello and sing.

Benjamin Franklin and Thomas Jefferson are the most well known examples of multi-talented Americans of this period whose skills included musical expertise. But there were others. Francis Hopkinson, a Philadelphian, signed the Declaration of Independence and was a very well known statesman, lawyer, and poet. He was also an organist and harpsichordist of great talent. A passionate and deeply committed musician, he was one of the new nation's very first composers. Among his works is a cycle of eight songs for voice and piano (or harpsichord) which he dedicated and sent to his friend, George Washington.[101] Hopkinson also sent several copies of the songs to Jefferson in December, 1788, when Jefferson was in Paris, along with a letter begging "Miss Jefferson's Acceptance of a Copy."[102]

Jefferson and Hopkinson often exchanged letters on musical subjects. From them, we know that Hopkinson found a new way to "quill" a harpsichord, referring to the "plectrum" which plucks the strings producing the instrument's sound. He also added a keyboard to Benjamin Franklin's glass-harmonica. Hopkinson's death in May, 1791, at the relatively young age of 54, was a great loss for his friends, his country, and for the future of American music.

As Secretary of State, Jefferson tried to negotiate the removal of British troops from below the Great Lakes, but his repeated efforts to conclude an agreement were frustrated by the Secretary of the Treasury, Alexander Hamilton, who had close connections with British financial interests. An ideological abyss separated these two men. Hamilton was a brilliant speaker and gifted writer with burning ambition. Jefferson and Jeffersonians saw him as motivated by self-interest. The feud between Jefferson and Hamilton became public and worsened. By September, 1792, Washington himself was concerned. These turbulent years did not leave much time for playing the violin, even if his wrist injury had not been a barrier.

In 1793, Jefferson cautiously watched the war between France and England. Later in the same year, anxious to escape the "tumult and shouting," he resigned as Secretary of State and returned to Monticello to farm and to oversee his new nail-making enterprise. In spite of careful bookkeeping he was in debt and needed additional revenues to meet expenses.

But Jefferson remained nonetheless dedicated to the life of the mind. To his delight, he

---

[101] The first American President thanked him with a gracious note expressing regret that he could "neither sing one of the songs, nor raise a single note on any instrument to convince the unbelieving." George Washington to Francis Hopkinson, 5 Feb. 1789, W.W. Abbott, ed. et al. *The Papers of George Washington, Presidential Series*, 8 vols. (Charlottesville: UP of Virginia, 1987-1999), 1:279–280.

[102] Francis Hopkinson to Thomas Jefferson, 1 Dec 1788, *Papers*, 14:324.

was elected President of the American Philosophical Society, a non-political office he held continuously from 1797 to 1815, even during his two terms as President of the United States. The Society, modeled on the Royal Society of London, was first organized by Benjamin Franklin in 1743 to expand American knowledge of the arts, natural sciences, technology and commerce. At its core was an elite circle of Jeffersonians upon whom Jefferson relied for advice and support: David Rittenhouse, astronomer; Dr. Benjamin Rush, physician and teacher; Benjamin Smith Barton, botanist; Joseph Priestly, chemist, physicist and religious philosopher; Charles Willson Peale, painter; and Thomas Paine, publicist and political writer.[103]

Mr. Jefferson re-entered the political fray, however, when his party nominated him for the Presidency in 1796. In a close and bitter contest, he lost to his former friend and diplomatic colleague, John Adams. Under the U.S. Constitution at that time the candidate receiving the second highest number of votes in the presidential election became Vice President, a position even less agreeable then than in our day. In an April, 1796 letter to a long-standing Italian friend then living in Florence, Italy, Philip Mazzei, Jefferson insulted the Hamiltonian-Adams opposition, describing it as "an Anglican monarchical & aristocratical party" which ignores Republican [i.e., Jeffersonian] values.[104] The letter became public. Jefferson had probably thought that the relatively innocuous Vice Presidency would be a haven from political gales, but now he found himself again in the eye of a storm. Then in 1801, after an arduous and mudslinging campaign, he took office as President. During his two presidential terms he was forced to spend more time than any music-lover would have preferred in Washington, D.C., the uninhabited area that had been selected for the national capital.

As the nineteenth century dawned, Philadelphia continued as the center of American music. In contrast, the nation's new capital was a sleepy little town with three taverns and no bookshops. Jefferson was accustomed to living in an unfinished house at Monticello, so the President's House, under construction at the time, was probably not as irritating for him as was the infrequency of worthwhile musical performances. Jefferson was accustomed to a much richer musical environment.

As indicated above, we have little evidence that he played his violin during these turbulent years. The burdens of his office and the continuing stiffness and discomfort in his injured right wrist were probably insurmountable impediments to serious playing, and the scarcity of musical performances must have saddened him. However, we know that Jefferson participat-

---

[103] Daniel J. Boorstin, *The Lost World of Thomas Jefferson* (Chicago: UP of Chicago, 1981), 8–26.
[104] Thomas Jefferson to Philip Mazzei, 24 Apr 1796, Library of Congress, Philip Mazzei Papers.

ed in dancing assemblies,[105] and the Philadelphia Opera Company sometimes staged productions in Washington. His old Philadelphia friend, Alexander Reinagle, would bring his large company, seventy members including twenty instrumentalists, to perform there.

The Third President of the United States may not have been pleased with the quality of the U.S. Marine Band that played at his 1801 inauguration. Lieutenant Colonel William Ward Burrows, the U.S. Marine Corps Commandant, had organized the Band just one year earlier.[106] The exact role Jefferson played in improving the U.S. Marine Band is unsubstantiated, but it seems that he and Colonel Burrows may have gone on a horseback ride, and, while they were alone, he encouraged the Commandant to improve the Band.[107] Especially after his Paris experiences, Jefferson may have reasoned that many of the Continent's finest musicians were from Italy, so he well could have suggested that the Colonel recruit in that part of Europe to bring bandsmen to Washington, which, in fact, did happen. In 1805 fourteen musicians from Palermo, accompanied by their families and newly-purchased instruments, immigrated to Washington, D.C. to become U.S. Marine bandsmen. Colonel Burrows' successor, without having been informed beforehand that foreign musicians were being recruited, eventually accommodated his Commander-in-Chief and integrated the Sicilians into the Band. But Washington, D.C. was decidedly not the thriving metropolis that most of this group of Europeans had anticipated. Eight returned home, but six remained to become leaders in the organization. Jefferson's account books during his presidency include frequent payments to the Band's music fund.[108] Since Jefferson's time, the U.S. Marine Band has set an example for similar musical organizations in the rest of the nation.

When Jefferson finally came home to Monticello in 1809, only Patsy, her family, and the plantation staff were there. She adored her father and saw to the household and the education of her many offspring under his watchful supervision. All of Patsy's children, particularly the girls, Anne Cary, Ellen, Cornelia, Virginia, Mary, and Septimia, were musical. Ellen was described as especially gifted on the harpsichord. Jefferson had purchased a valuable Spanish guitar for Virginia, who also played the piano and sang. The grandchildren adored their "Grand-Papa" and he, in turn, was happiest when surrounded by them. Now freed from

---

[105] During his presidency, Thomas Jefferson had memberships in three "dancing assemblies:" the Washington Dancing Assembly, the Georgetown Dancing Assembly and a dancing assembly held at Stelle's Hotel. See *Memorandum & Account Books*, 2:1059, 1087, 1088, 1118, 1144, 1153, 1168, 1197, 1215, 1217. The subject is also discussed in Cripe, 26.

[106] Edwin N. McClellan, "How The Marine Band Started," *Proceedings*, U.S. Naval Institute (Annapolis: April, 1923), 582–83.

[107] Cripe, 24–6.

[108] See, e.g., *Memorandum & Account Books*, 2:1143, n32.

the demands of public office, the elder statesman enjoyed evenings of music and socializing with Patsy and her family at Monticello.

Jefferson's Violins and Bows

In addition to a harpsichord and a guitar, there were several violins at Monticello. It is regrettable and somewhat puzzling that while Jefferson was deeply committed to the violin, he wrote practically nothing about the instruments he owned. We know about his kit violin, the practice instrument that he carried with him in his early days as a lawyer, because he referred to the saddle enclosure he designed to protect it during his early years traveling to and from Williamsburg. We also know about three more violins that he purchased after his 25th year, which implies that he owned others, because he had been playing since childhood. The three we know about were itemized in his memorandum and account books.

On May 25, 1768, he paid a Dr. Pasteur of Williamsburg £5 for one which Jefferson thereafter called his "Cremona."[109] This instrument of Jefferson's might well have claimed an Amati pedigree. Nicolo Amati and other members of his family were famous for the violins they made at the Italian city of Cremona during the sixteenth and seventeenth centuries.[110] The renowned Antonio Stradivari was one of Amati's apprentices. Along with instruments by Stradivari, and other outstanding makers like members of the Guarneri family, Amati violins were then, as now, sought-after because of their silvery, soprano quality. Amati violins had an arched back and a short neck which, in more recent years, have been lengthened to accommodate the higher registers. The Stradivari violins, with their large, beautiful tone, are more suited for present-day concert halls and for playing concerti. Stradivari, as well as the Guarneri violins and similar instruments, have a flattened back and longer necks.

The violin bow has changed a great deal over the centuries. Arcangelo Corelli (1653–1713), one of the pillars of Italian violin music and performance, used a shorter bow than the twentieth-century version. It had a slight outward (convex) curve.

Because the convex bow was fashionable until relatively late in Jefferson's life, it is probable that he used this type. Bows arrived at their present shape largely due to the influence of François Tourte (1747–1835), a Parisian who worked on the bow shape for some sixty years, 1770–1830.[111] In contrast to the Corelli type, the bow Tourte perfected was longer and

---

[109] *Memorandum & Account Books*, 1:77.

[110] Nicolo Amati (1596–1684) was the greatest in a family of violin makers working in Cremona, Italy. In his studio and working under his supervision were later legendary makers: Stradivari, Guarneri del Gesú, Ruggeri, and others.

[111] David D. Boyden, "Tourte," *New Grove Dictionary*, 19:100.

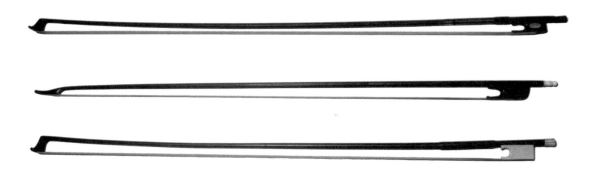

FIGURE 7. *Three violin bows of types in use during the 18th century. The top item is an English pre-Tourte bow with a modern concave design. In the middle is shown a modern copy by Louis Begin of an early 18th century (so-called "Corelli" style) bow, clearly showing its convex profile and somewhat shorter length. The bottom item is, again, an English pre-Tourte concave bow, in this instance with an ivory "frog." (Courtesy of the Harry R. Lange Historical Collection of Musical Instruments and Books, Stanford University, and Mr. Herbert Myers, Curator.)*

curved inward, toward the strings, enabling the player to produce a *cantilena*, a singing style, as well as greater dynamic nuances. A Tourte bow attributed to Jefferson's violin collection appeared at a New York City exhibition in 1971.[112]

François Tourte was making his bows while Jefferson was a diplomat in Paris. Although Jefferson very likely played with a convex bow, it is also possible that the innovatively-designed Tourte bow was among the many European technical, artistic, and literary treasures he shipped back to Virginia. Acquisition of a Tourte-style bow would have been consistent with Jefferson's unbounded commitment to new inventions, despite his (by then) almost-crippled right wrist.

Seven years after the "Cremona" purchase in 1768, Jefferson paid £13, a bargain price, for another fine Italian violin. It has been referred to as his "Randolph" violin by historians because the acquisition of it stemmed from a series of events involving John Randolph of Williamsburg. Randolph, appointed by the Crown as Attorney General of the Virginia Royal Colony, was Jefferson's friend and a violinist as well. The two of them frequently played together. Jefferson loved Randolph's beautiful violin, and Randolph admired Jefferson's extensive library. In 1771 the two young men entered into a unique (and probably somewhat facetious) agreement before seven witnesses, one of whom was George Wythe, and acknowledged the contract before a judge. (The contract is reproduced in full in Appendix 1 of this mono-

---

[112] Cripe, 132.

graph.)[113] According to the document, which was "recorded" in the Virginia General Court, if Jefferson survived Randolph, the violin "together with all [Randolph's] music composed for the violin" would be Jefferson's, or he would receive books from Randolph's estate worth £60 if the music (and the violin?) had been "destroyed." If Jefferson predeceased him, Randolph would receive a selection of books from Jefferson's library of a value of £100.

By 1775 the political climate in the Virginia Colony had changed, and with it, their friendship. Randolph was a British loyalist—a Tory—and, as the antipathy between revolutionaries and Tories heated up, Randolph thought it wise to leave Virginia and go to England. The agreement was dissolved, but, before Randolph left, the violin was offered for sale to Jefferson through a third party. In spite of his obsessive bookkeeping, Jefferson was not an efficient money manager. However, he was not oblivious to a good bargain: according to their original contract, Randolph's offer gave Jefferson the chance to acquire this violin for approximately a third of its value, some £13.[114] To be sure, the Louisiana Purchase was not the only good bargain Jefferson managed to negotiate!

His account books also inform us that in 1788 he purchased "a small violin" in Paris, and it appears that it may have been another *pochette* or kit.[115] We do know that he kept the two Italian violins throughout his life. After Jefferson's death in 1826 the family asked Joseph Coolidge, Jefferson's grandson-in-law, to sell them. Mr. Coolidge sent them to London, one of the best markets, then as now, for fine string instruments. Unfortunately, we do not know what became of them after that. Jefferson family records are silent on the matter. But does the story end there? The Thomas Jefferson Memorial Foundation has examined dozens of claims about instruments allegedly belonging to the Master of Monticello. So far, none has proved to be genuine, but 200 years in the life of a great violin is not long. Is it only wishful thinking to imagine that one day a violin actually owned and played by Jefferson might be identified?

Jefferson's Library & the Italian Violin School

When we study Jefferson's music library catalogue (part of his larger 1783 Monticello library catalogue), we find music instruction books, often called "tutors," giving pointers on how to sing and how to play instruments.[116] Francesco Geminiani's *The Art of Playing on The*

---

[113] The complete text of this contract (reproduced herein in Appendix 1) can be found in *Papers*, 1:66–7.

[114] *Memorandum & Account Books*, 1:405.

[115] "This was a *pochette* or kit which [Jefferson] used for practice and later gave to a student at the University of Virginia." The price was 36 livres. *Memorandum & Account Books*, 1:712, n. 8.

[116] Please see Appendix 2 to this essay for an extract from Jefferson's 1783 library catalogue.

Violin, part of the 1783 listing, is among the most important violin tutors of the eighteenth century.[117] Geminiani's book, and another method book by Leopold Mozart (father of Wolfgang), *Versuch einer gründlichen Violinschule* ("Essay on the Fundamental Principles of Violin Technique"),[118] were the most important printed resources with which eighteenth-century professional violinists honed advanced performance techniques.

Geminiani (1687–1762) was a violinist-composer, teacher, and theorist who lived and worked in London during most of the first half of the eighteenth century. His method was novel; it was intended for professional players. Geminiani emphasized a close relationship between artist-teacher and pupil.

Jefferson must have studied Geminiani's book in his usual intensive manner, because he himself annotated it. At the bottom of page 8 of his own copy of *The Art of Playing on the Violin*[119] Jefferson quoted almost verbatim, in his own hand, Dr. Burney's footnoted comment in *The Present State of Music in France and Italy*[120] on the "close shake," a subject Geminiani addresses (at the top of page 8 of *The Art of Playing on the Violin*). Jefferson's note looks like this:

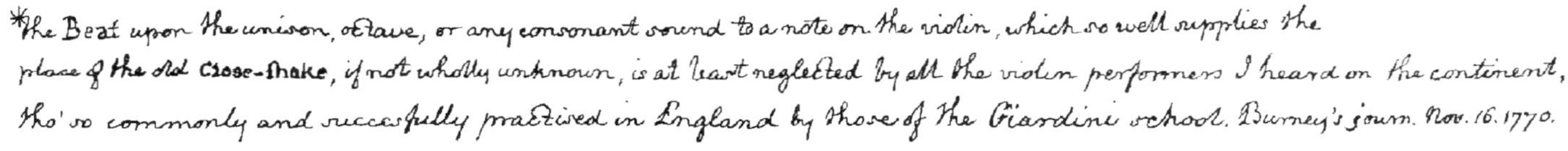

The Beat upon the unison, octave, or any consonant sound to a note on the violin, which so well supplies the place of the old Close-shake, if not wholly unknown, is at least neglected by all the violin performers I heard on the continent, tho' so commonly and successfully practised in England by those of the Giardini school. Burney's journ. Nov. 16. 1770.

FIGURE 8. *Thomas Jefferson's Annotation to page 8 of The Art of Playing on the Violin.(Courtesy of Library of Congress, Thomas Jefferson Collection, Washington, D.C.)*

This handwritten annotation[121] is revealing because it demonstrates that Jefferson was interested in the technical problems of the vibrato, but at a level far above the standards of a beginner or amateur violinist.

Playing the violin is an exhilarating affair, where each arm and each hand plays its indi-

---

[117] Francesco Geminiani, *The Art of Playing on the Violin* (London: 1751). Fr. trans., 1752; Ger. trans. (with changes), Vienna, 1785(?).

[118] Leopold Mozart, *Versuch einer gründlichen Violinschule* (Augsburg: 1756). Dutch trans., 1766; Fr. trans., 1770; and numerous other unauthorized reprintings and edns.

[119] Jefferson's copy of Geminiani's instruction book, which is part of the Thomas Jefferson Collection of the Library of Congress, was originally part of his personal library which was sold to Congress in 1815, several years after the Library of Congress was burned by the British in the War of 1812. The volume survived the Christmas Day, 1851 fire that destroyed much of the Library of Congress and a large part of the Jefferson library.

[120] Burney, *The Present State of Music in France and Italy*, facsimile ed, footnote on pages 388–89.

[121] Jefferson's handwriting reads: "*The Beat upon the unison, octave, or any consonant sound to a note on the violin, which so well supplies the place of the old Close-shake, if not wholly unknown, is at least neglected by all the violin performers I heard on the continent, tho' so commonly and successfully practiced in England by those of the Giardini school. Burney's journ. Nov. 16, 1770.*" [Actually, the source of the quote is from *Burney*, November *18, 1770.*]

vidual role. As the violin teacher L'Abbé le Fils once said, "The bow is the soul of the instrument."[122] The right (i.e., "bow") arm, supplemented by the right wrist, creates musical sound by drawing the bow hairs across the strings. The right hand and wrist transmit and at the same time refine the pressure of the right arm; the index finger of the right hand helps to regulate the weight, thereby controlling the volume and intensity of the tone, while the right thumb and the other fingers are engaged in the delicate role of holding and balancing the bow. The left arm serves as a foundation. The left hand and fingers supply the pitch of the sound with "fingerings" that move back and forth over the violin's neck in various "positions" and creates tonal "colors" through vibrato, which Geminiani, on page 8 of *The Art of Playing on the Violin*, seems to termed "the close-shake."[123]

In Jefferson's day, the *vibrato* was modest and infrequently employed. The modern so-called "continuous vibrato" did not become the norm until Fritz Kreisler made it so, in the twentieth century. Two types of vibrato in the eighteenth-century violinist's technical repertory were: (1) the "true" vibrato in which one finger undulates the pitch above *and below* the given note with the wrist in order to color the tone; and (2) the two-finger method which, according to David Boyden, Geminiani calls the "close shake." Boyden describes this method succinctly:

> [O]ne finger is pressed firmly on the fret and a second finger makes a rapid beating or shaking very close to the pressed-down first finger (hence the name 'close shake'). Actually this type of vibrato is not a true vibrato at all. It is really a species of trill. . . .[124]

Jefferson was clearly interested in *vibrato* and similar musical special effects. That he had

Jefferson's handwriting on the document was examined and authenticated by Dr. Douglas L. Wilson, Saunders Director, International Center for Jefferson Studies, Thomas Jefferson Foundation, Charlottesville, Virginia: "There is not a doubt in the world that this is Jefferson's handwriting. What is more, this handwriting has all the characteristics of the hand Jefferson employed in the early 1770s." Personal communication with this writer, 29 Sept. 1997.

[122] L'Abbé le fils (Joseph Barnabé Saint-Sévin) (d. 1803), composer and superb violinist, member of the concert spirituel and the Paris Opéra orchestra. He is remembered chiefly for his violin method, *Principes du violon* (Paris: 1761), which, after Leopold Mozart's *Versüch* and Geminiani's *Art of Playing on the Violin*, was the most important method of the day. His innovations included use of half and second positions, harmonics, double stops, and holding the violin in the modern way. See Boyden, David D., *The History of Playing the Violin from Its Origins to 1761* (London: Oxford UP, 1990), 359–60.

[123] The execution of rapid scale passages and double, triple, and quadruple "stops"—or chords—belongs to left-hand technique, although the last two were played, until the nineteenth century, with the right hand's help, *arpeggiato* or "harp-like."

[124] Boyden, *History*, 288.

read and remembered Burney's book well enough to reproduce verbatim an obscure footnote on a highly technical point found in the very last portion of the volume and write it into his copy of *The Art of Playing on the Violin* strongly suggests Jefferson's fascination with the niceties of eighteenth-century violin technique.

The Art of Playing on the Violin was well known and studied by violinists all over Europe, as its numerous reprints, translations, and imitations by other authors and publishers testify. In several other treatises Geminiani emphasized the importance of expressive quality in violin playing by dynamic shadings (*crescendo, diminuendo, messa di voce*), ornamentation, and a type of continuous vibrato which he used in his own performance.[125] He applied his emphasis on expression in his well-known published ornamentation of Corelli's Sonata for Violin and Continuo, Op. 5, No. 9 in D Major.[126] Geminiani's own twelve Opus 1 sonatas demand no small measure of virtuosity from the performer: an extended range, skips, multiple stops, challenging passage-work, and sophisticated bowings. It seems likely that Jefferson played some of Geminiani's works, all of which require considerable technical skill, even today.

Many works for both violin and *continuo* and violin and orchestra by Italian baroque masters are listed in Jefferson's 1783 music library catalog; in fact, more than half of the instrumental works listed there are by Italian composers.[127] Italian musicians abound in Jefferson's library because, after the creation of operatic culture in the seventeenth century, Italy assumed a leading role in the world of European music. By the beginning of the eighteenth century, Italian music, especially Italian violin music, was everywhere—in the theater, in the church (*sonata da chiesa*), at soirées (*sonata da camera*), and at princely and royal courts throughout Europe. At that time it was axiomatic that Italian composers had a gift for the *cantabile* ("singing") style. The performance practice and the compositions of what can rightfully be called the Italian Violin School were the foundations of Jefferson's musical education and experience.

At the center of Italian music for the violin in the eighteenth century was the violin sonata, a musical genre originally of the sixteenth and seventeenth centuries and shaped into

---

[125] Although Geminiani was a student of Corelli's and was Italian by birth, his career flourished in England where he went in 1715 after Corelli's death. His recitals immediately drew the admiration of musicians and the aristocracy. Dr. Burney praised his overwhelming technical audacity. His tempestuous playing had already earned him the epithet "*Il Furibondo*" ("the wrathful one") from Tartini. Among other of Geminiani's publications was *Rules for Playing in True Taste on the Violin*, Op. VIII, London, 1739.

[126] Printed by Hawkins in 1776. See *New Grove Dictionary*, 7:224.

[127] Alphabetically those composers were: Battino, Bezossi, Boccherini, Borghi, Campioni, Corelli, Degiardino (another name for Giardini), Figlio, Gasparini, Giardini, Geminiani, Lampugnani, Martini, Pasquali, Pergolesi, Pugnani, Tessarini, and Vivaldi. Appendix 2 sets forth Jefferson's listing in full.

an attractive form by the renowned violinist Arcangelo Corelli,[128] a Bologna-trained virtuoso who settled in Rome. The *sonata* (Italian, *suonare*, to sound) became, by the first decade of the eighteenth century, an instrumental composition written most typically for a string or wind player accompanied by a harpsichordist and cellist (the *basso continuo*), and organized into several sections or "movements." In Corelli's violin sonatas, the number of movements varied: there were between five and seven, each based upon different dance rhythms, thus contrasting in character, with the tempo of successive movements alternating between slow and fast. The noble and thoughtful introductory movement was, as a rule, slow. Under Corelli's hand the sonata gained further emotional depth through the use of ingeniously varied dynamics (loud and soft passages). Corelli also enriched virtually all his slow movements with elaborate ornamentation: trills, turns, appogiaturas and arpeggios. Musically literate violinists of Jefferson's day—and Jefferson was beyond dispute a musically literate violinist—looked upon Corelli's sonatas as a kind of musical Bible, in much the same way as, for example, pianists today regard J.S. Bach's *Well-Tempered Clavier* and Beethoven's 32 piano sonatas.

Editions and reprints of Corelli's violin sonatas poured forth from the music publishers of the day, carrying the composer's name and compositions all over Europe and England—and thence to America. Corelli's sonatas found an honored place in Jefferson's 1783 library catalog, with no fewer than four separate entries. It must have been great fun for the Master of Monticello and the lady of the house to play Corelli's music; it was not too difficult, seldom requiring the violinist to shift his left hand up the instrument's neck beyond the third position.

What was Corelli like when playing?[129] David Boyden quotes a contemporary source

I never met with any man who suffered his passions to hurry him away so much whilst he was playing on the violin as the famous Arcangelo Corelli, whose eyes will sometimes turn

---

[128] Corelli was one of the most important violinist-composer-teachers of the seventeenth century. He was called "father" of the Italian violinists and "founder" of the Bologna-Rome violin school. Though he wore the mantle of the earlier Bolognese masters, from age eighteen he worked in Rome and lived at the palace of his friend, Cardinal Pietro Ottoboni. Roman society flocked to Corelli's concerts. Although his compositional output was limited, its influence was enormous. His few compositions were centered on the violin; these consisted principally of solo sonatas and trio-sonatas for two violins and *basso continuo* (played by harpsichord and cello). Jefferson must have studied Corelli's music and very probably performed it before he went to Paris.

[129] Corelli is reputed to have owned and performed on two different violins: the first by Andrea Amati, a celebrated Cremonese maker (father of Nicola), the other by Matthias Albani, who, like Jacob Stainer, was a Austrian master *luthier* from the Tyrol. These instruments had relatively short necks and arched backs, the basic design emphasizing beauty and sweetness of tone, and achieving these admirable qualities at some expense to the carrying power of the sound. (Boyden, *History*, 195) As as been mentioned, one of Jefferson's instruments, the "Cremona," may well have been an Amati.

as red as fire; his countenance will be distorted, his eyeballs roll as in an agony, and he gives in so much to what he is doing that he doth not look like the same man.[130]

Although this level of emotionalism is somewhat surprising given Corelli's reportedly amiable and dignified nature, his fervor while playing was quite in accord with the *Zeitgeist* of the Baroque. Did Jefferson experience something of this same sort of emotional intensity when he had a violin under his bow?

In addition to his pioneering work on the *sonata*, which was, of course, a small-scale composition intended for more intimate venues and occasions, Corelli also composed *concerti*, a form which deploys more extensive musical forces. It was concert music which expressed the Baroque's love for drama and conflict, and it was, most particularly, "concerted" music—that is, music in the *concerto* form, emphasizing conflict between contrasting tonal groups—by which Corelli and his musical successors[131] enthralled their large concert audiences.[132]

---

[130] François Raguenet, "Comparison Between French and Italian Music," (1702) English translation attributed to J.E. Galliard (1709). Reprinted in *The Musical Quarterly*, July, 1946, p. 419, n. 15, quoted in Boyden, *History*, 243.

[131] Among Corelli's outstanding students was G.B. Somis (1686-1763), who later founded a school in Torino, in turn influencing Felice Giardini (1716–1796) and Gaetano Pugnani (1731–1798), these latter two violinists and composers being represented in Jefferson's library. Pietro Locatelli (1695–1764), one of the most admired violinists of the first half of the eighteenth century, had his training in Rome, possibly by Corelli. After many tours he settled in Amsterdam. He is sometimes called "the Paganini of the eighteenth century" because of his sensational technical prowess. As a composer, his sonatas and solo concerti contributed significantly to the development of these musical forms. Locatelli owned and played both Jacob Stainer and Amati violins. Another Corelli follower, Francesco Maria Veracini (1690–1768) was another of the great violin virtuosi of the time. His successes took him to the courts of Dresden and to London, where he was later eclipsed by Geminiani. Veracini was admired for his beautiful tone. According to Burney his violins were a pair of Jacob Stainers, which he named "Saint Peter" and "Saint Paul." Veracini's best known—and finest—work was his *Sonate accademiche* for violino solo, Op. 2, published in London in 1744. An engraved portrait of Veracini playing the violin is to be found in that work and is shown as Fig. 9. This image shows the standard eighteenth-century method of holding the instrument, most likely the way Jefferson held it.

[132] Twentieth-century performance practice calls for small forces in performing Baroque music, which is historically correct. However, there is also a monumental aspect to Baroque music. When Corelli led an orchestra often a large number of players participated. For example, at concerts given in February, 1687, at the Roman *palazzo* of his early patron, Christina, Queen of Sweden, Corelli led an orchestra of 150 string players and 100 singers. (Michael Talbot, "Corelli," *New Grove Dictionary*, 6: 769). Geminiani observed that Corelli introduced bowing discipline at rehearsals and, that, as a leader, he insisted on the precise execution of down and up bows, so all bows in each section would be played together. [Charles Burney, *A General History of Music*, Vol. II, Reprinted Ed., New York 1935, 443; quoted in Boyden, *History*, 257] We could well imagine that the sight and sound of all this was breathtaking, much like listening to a great, sophisticated twentieth-century orchestra. The orchestral culture that Corelli nurtured spread quickly all over Europe and to England. The court of Karl Theodor, Elector of the Rhine Palatinate at Mannheim, had an exceptionally fine orchestra which elicited great admiration from the young Mozart. The famed Parisian concert spirituel orchestra, whose concerts Jefferson attended frequently during his five years in Paris, was also noted for its disciplined string playing.

Corelli's concertos, *including the individual parts for the orchestra*, were also a key part of Jefferson's personal Monticello music collection.[133]

The word *concerto* derives from the Italian (and Latin) *concertare*: to fight, to vie with one other. There are two unequal tonal masses. In the *concerto grosso*, the only type of concerto that Corelli composed, a small group of players, the *concertino* or solo group (usually two violins and a cello) is pitted against a larger group, the *ripieno* (the "full", frequently also called the "*tutti*" ("all"), i.e., the remaining players, including a basso continuo). Though their numbers are unequal, the musical roles of the two concerting groups are equal. Their individual character lies in contrasting dynamics (i.e., loudness and softness),

FIGURE 9 *Engraved portrait of Francesco Maria Veraccini from his Sonnate accademiche, 1744*

differing tone color (timbre), and the use of higher as opposed to lower registers. The obligatory, omnipresent harpsichord—the heart of the basso continuo— supplied harmonic support and helped hold the ensemble together rhythmically. The concerto grosso form was further developed by Corelli's followers and quickly spread to France, to German-speaking lands, and to England. Corelli wrote only twelve posthumously-published *concerti grossi;* he did not write any concertos for solo instruments. That latter form was developed by, among others, Albinoni, Torelli, and Locatelli, and then brought to new heights by the renowned Venetian composer, Antonio Vivaldi,[134] several of whose works, both sonatas and concertos, were an integral part of Jefferson's music collection.

In his solo concertos Vivaldi had many imaginative solutions for the concerto's musical challenges. His work established the concerto as a three-movement composition in a fixed tempo sequence: fast, slow, fast. Vivaldi usually began his violin concertos with a short, bold,

---

[133] It is intriguing to ask: Why would Jefferson buy individual orchestra parts? Who would play them? This brings us back to our earlier conjecture: did the Master of Monticello have plans to have a "house orchestra" (perhaps on the model of Prince Nicolaus, "The Magnificent", Eszterházy) in which Jefferson and his wife might actively participate? See pages 12–14 above, discussing the Fabbroni letter of 1778.

[134] Born in Venice and working there almost all his life, Antonio Vivaldi (1676–1741) became one of the most important composers of his time. While still in his youth after a short period as an ordained priest (he was called *il prete rosso*, "the red priest," because of his hair color), he turned to his real calling: music. He was amazingly prolific. Vivaldi composed more than 230 concertos for the violin alone (!) as well as hundreds of other concertos, sonatas, cantatas, and some forty-five operas. His was a strikingly original and brilliant mind with a flair for experimentation.

strongly rhythmic theme which immediately captured the listeners' attention, oftentimes following it with a warm, lyric melody which anticipated the singing allegros of Mozart.[135] The challenge for the composer of a solo concerto is to reconcile the *concerto principle*—the good-natured combat of equally important tonal forces—with the fact that in a solo concerto there is only a single instrument contesting with the many.[136] In striking a balance between very unequal forces, but at the same time having to dramatize this struggle as between musical equals, Vivaldi also gave the violin soloist brilliant, virtuoso passages in the higher registers, music that an ordinary member of the orchestra would find technically beyond his or her capability. As developed by Vivaldi, another method of promoting aesthetic balance in solo concertos was structural, i.e., the use of the *ritornello*, "little return", in which the orchestra states the theme, the soloist restating it with elaboration. The orchestra, also called the *tutti*, returns with the theme and, after a few dialogues between soloist and orchestra involving key changes (i.e, modulations), the movement ends, often with soloist and orchestra playing together to a resounding conclusion.

THE JEFFERSON FAMILY MUSIC COLLECTION

In the University of Virginia's Alderman Library we can see what remains of the Jefferson family's music collection, now the property of the Thomas Jefferson Foundation, Inc. According to Professor Ronald Kidd of Purdue University, only about ten percent of Jefferson's and his family's original collection remains.[137] A servant of a Jefferson descendant burned most of the music to start a fire in a household stove. With probably all good intentions the servant may have assumed that used sheet music was not valuable, but that old newspapers, which the family saved, might have some historical value, so they—not the music—were preserved.[138]

---

[135] Vivaldi's melodic gifts remind us that he was also an opera composer. And his violinist's imagination contributed some original effects, like the *bariolage*, a brisk changing of two strings, one stopped, the other unstopped (open). As for innovative bowing, Boyden (*History*, at 475) quotes an absolutely mesmerizing passage from the second movement of Vivaldi's *Concerto for Four Violins* in b minor, Op. 10 no. 3, where the four soloists play arpeggios together, each with different bowings. As a composer, violinist, and teacher, Vivaldi was one of the principal representatives of the great Italian violin school. In his love of drama and tonal color he is a true son of his native city, joining the great Venetian painters and musicians as an immortal.

[136] It is worth noting, too, that as concerts moved from aristocratic salons out to the public, and larger concert halls with larger orchestras confronted violin soloists, these soloists needed more powerful instruments. The great Amati and Stainer instruments, despite their silvery and beautiful tone, did not meet the new conditions. It remained to Antonio Stradivari of Cremona (1644–1737) who, along with other Cremonese masters, to create the longer-necked, flatter-backed instruments that had the requisite power and beauty of tone.

[137] Personal communication with this writer, dated August 26, 1997.

[138] Marie Kimball, *Road to Glory*, 59.

The extant Jefferson Family Music Collection consists of mostly secular works. The scores that remain are classified as vocal and instrumental pieces.[139] In carefully organized and preserved folders are songs, exercises from instruction books, sonatas, ballad operas, operatic arias, pieces for the harpsichord, arrangements and miscellany. In addition to the printed editions, we find books filled with manuscript copies of favorites. Reminiscent of the J.S. Bach family, Jefferson's progeny seemed to have contributed lovingly to its family's musical treasures. Among the annotations to these music scores we find the handwriting of Jefferson himself; his wife, Martha Wayles Jefferson; his daughters Martha (Patsy) Jefferson Randolph and Mary (Maria) Jefferson; and, very likely, his granddaughters, Ellen Randolph Coolidge, Virginia Randolph Trist, and Septimia Randolph Meikleham.

We can reasonably infer from a sonata in a surviving, well-thumbed and annotated copy of Corelli's Op. 5 sonatas for violin and continuo in the Jefferson Family Music Collection, in d minor and titled "La Follia", that Jefferson was (before his wrist injury) able to perform the complex bowing demanded by late seventeenth- and eighteenth-century violin compositions.[140] The terminology describing these bow-strokes is mostly Italian in the Corelli tradition, or French from French dance music, later extensively developed by the French Violin School. "La Follia," set of some 20 variations on a Spanish-Portuguese melody, is a treasure-trove of eighteenth-century violin techniques. For bowing strokes it includes:

- *Détaché with separate strokes*, both down-bow and up-bow used in fairly rapid movement;
- *Détaché mixed with slurs*, a favorite virtuoso bowing method used by Viotti in Paris;
- *Martelé*, a forceful *staccato* stroke with down- and up-bow;[141]
- *Slurred Staccato*, a *staccato* stroke comprising several notes sounding separately and detached on one bow, a difficult maneuver usually played up-bow;
- *Sautillé*, an indication for separate strokes, the bow being lifted for each stroke;
- *Double Stops*, consisting of two notes (i.e., strings) played simultaneously;
- *Triple and Quadruple Stops*, a challenge to both hands because they were played *arpeggiato* (i.e., arpeggiated).

"La Follia" requires an expressive style of playing, typical of what the Italian violin composers from Corelli through Geminiani expected. Apparently, Jefferson played this repertory. Again, this suggests his expertise on the instrument.

It is surprising to find several works by Carlo Antonio Campioni (1720–1788) listed in

---

[139] A listing of the composers and compositions represented in the Jefferson Family Music Collection is contained at the end of this essay in Appendix 3.

[140] Examples of many of these bowings and to be found in Corelli's "La Follia" appear in Appendix 6.

[141] The use of *martelé* was more common in the second half of the eighteenth century than in the first.

FIGURE 10. *Jefferson's notation of opening bars of Campioni works. (Jefferson Family Music Collection, Alderman library, University of Virginia)*

Jefferson's 1783 catalogue. Another indication of Campioni's importance to Jefferson is contained on a small sheet of paper in the Jefferson Family Music Collection. On it we can see that, with his usual meticulous attention to detail and in his fine italic hand, Jefferson copied the opening measures of the Campioni compositions he possessed,[142] and then penned his desire to acquire more of them in a note on the paper to a music vendor in the following lines:[143]

Campioni, an Italian composer of French birth, was well-known in Jefferson's day. Charles Burney certainly knew his works, which were published in Paris, Amsterdam, and London. Burney may have known Campioni personally and he might well have acquainted his friend, Jefferson, with Campioni's music. Trained as a violinist by Tartini,[144] Campioni had been *Maestro di Capella* at the *cattedrale* in Livorno and, afterwards, the same post at Santa Maria delle Fiore, the *duomo* of Florence. He held a similar position at the Grand Ducal Court of Tuscany located in the Palazzo Pitti, where he wrote numerous ecclesiastical pieces. His more popular works, however, were for chamber ensembles and solo instruments.

---

[142] The reader should observe just how fluidly and neatly Jefferson wrote musical notation. Writing out music was obviously something with which he was quite familiar.

[143] Jefferson wrote: *On this paper is noted the beginning of the several compositions of Campioni which are in possession of T. Jefferson. He would be glad to have everything else he has composed of solos, duets, or trios. printed copies would be preferred, but if not to be had he would have them in manuscript.*

[144] Giuseppe Tartini (1692–1770) was an admired and respected Italian violinist, composer and theorist. Although he concertized all over Europe, his home was Padova. His *Trattato di musica secondo la vera scienza dell'armonia* of 1754 was influential. Tartini's epithet concerning Geminiani can be found in *New Grove Dictionary*, 7: 227.

These works included six sets of trio sonatas for two violins and *basso continuo*, six duets for violin and cello, Op. 7, and six duets for two violins, Op. 8. He also wrote six sonatas for solo harpsichord. All of these works were part of Jefferson's 1783 library. Like Jefferson's wife, Martha, Campioni's wife was a harpsichordist.

The influence of the famous eighteenth-century Bolognese music teacher and theorist, Padre Martini, may be observed in Campioni's music. In the trio-sonatas the texture tends to be contrapuntal, with the cello striving towards an independent line. Campioni's violin sonatas require an advanced technique. They demand, among other things, multiple stops (arpeggiated in the case of three or four-part chords), wide skips, varied and slurred bowing, and sudden shifts of left-hand position. They are certainly not easy to play.

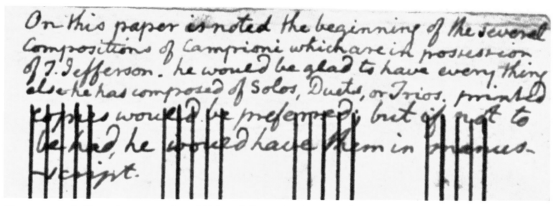

FIGURE II. *Jefferson's request for additional Campioni works. (Jefferson Family Music Collection, Alderman library, University of Virginia)*

CONCLUSIONS

According to Nicholas Trist, his grandson-in-law, Thomas Jefferson claimed to have practiced three hours daily for a "dozen years" during the 1760s and 1770s. Even if this might have been an exaggeration, the level of practice the comment suggests certainly conveys a very great commitment to and enjoyment of the violin. Jefferson was a passionate perfectionist, therefore no speculative leap is needed to conclude that when he turned to violin playing he would excel. Others described him as skilled beyond his amateur peers. Some of these descriptions came from other amateur violinists, including European aristocrats who had probably been exposed to at least some of Europe's great professional musicians of the era.

We have a listing and a few remnants of his extraordinary music library. Jefferson almost surely played some of the music in his library, and, as explained above, Corelli, Geminiani, and Campioni did not write for amateurs; their music demands the expertise of a professional. We can infer, therefore, that until he broke his wrist, Thomas Jefferson was an excellent violinist—and could well have been a professional musician, had not such a vocation been inappropriate for an eighteenth-century Virginia gentleman.[145]

Jefferson was a very private man. The more personal and emotionally-charged an issue, the less he said about it. He admitted, at least, that music was his "passion."[146] Music in general and the violin in particular were part of the inner, very personal, very reticent Jefferson— his emotional core that he consistently refused to expose to public scrutiny. Based on what we know about his activities, the importance of music to Jefferson is apparent, and his nearly complete silence about his feelings for music is similar to his silence about the other deeply-felt issues of his life.

When we try to probe behind his violin playing to music's role in his emotional being, that territory becomes obscure, by Jefferson's own design. "Music," he wrote, is the "favorite passion of my soul", a "delightful recreation", or "an enjoyment, the deprivation of which …. cannot be calculated." These words are just about the only statements about the meaning of music to Jefferson that come directly from him. In a way peculiar to Jefferson, his reticence to talk about the role of music in his life can be taken as proof of music's importance to him.

Jefferson's pattern was to trap the more emotional components of his existence within the rational boundaries of intellectual discourse. In addition, the more basic the component's emotional charge, the fewer words assigned. He used his dazzling social and verbal fluency in combination with selective silence to prevent the world from peeking behind his erudition and his worldly accomplishments. We can only surmise, for example, that the broken wrist was a turning point in his emotional life, because he never discussed (at least in writing) its implications for his violin playing. When dealing with political philosophy, Jefferson unleashed torrents of rational expression, but, when the subject turned to the source of these torrents, Jefferson became, to borrow Joseph Ellis' apt epithet for him, an "American Sphinx."

We can properly speculate, however, about Jefferson's use of the violin for emotional expression and self-support. As we are informed, he played the violin in times of joy as well

---

[145] "[In the eighteenth century] [g]entlemen amateurs, such as Jefferson and Francis Hopkinson, were very definitely gentlemen, no matter how good they were as musicians, and as gentlemen they could *never* appear in any situation that might imply that they were receiving pay for their services." [emphasis supplied] Cripe, 7.

[146] Abigail Adams, with her usual perspicacity, also recognized that music was Jefferson's "favorite passion." See note 56, above. Had she heard Jefferson describe the importance of music in his life using those exact words? Based on what we know about Jefferson's devotion to music and that he had used "favorite passion" in his correspondence to Fabbroni (see notes 34 and 35 above and related text), it would not seem too hazardous to answer the question in the affirmative.

as grief. The German poet, Heinrich Heine, succinctly expressed what violinists feel about playing their instrument:

Die Violine ist ein Instrument, welches fast menschliche Launen hat und mit der Stimmung des Spielers sozusagen in einem sympathischen Rapport steht: das geringste Mißbehagen, die leiseste Gemültserschütterung, ein Gefühlshauch, findet hier einen unmittelbaren Widerhall, und das kommt wohl daher, weil die Violine, so ganz nahe an unsere Brust gedrückt, auch unser Herzklopfen vernimmt.

(The violin is an instrument which possesses almost human temperament; it is attuned to the mood of the player in nearly sympathetic rapport: the slightest discomfort, the tiniest disturbance of disposition, a breath of emotion, finds an immediate echo, and that is because the violin, pressed so near our breast, senses our heart's beating.)[147]

Playing the violin apparently gave comfort to Jefferson. He must have been closely attuned to his violin and, when it was at one with the beat of his heart, seen it as an extension of his body and spirit, a most personal and private form of expression.

The noted violin pedagogue, Carl Flesch, once explained to this writer that when violinists hold the instrument between the chin and collarbone, they feel the instrument as a continuation, an integral part of their bodies. When drawing the bow across the strings the instrument not only resonates, but the human body reverberates as well. Violin playing, Flesch concluded, provides immense satisfaction for the player. Some great violinists of the past—including Heifetz, Huberman, and Kreisler—have used such terms as "emotional release." Although Jefferson may not have performed at the level of a professional violinist, playing the violin almost certainly provided him tremendous emotional release and must have occupied a central place in his heart for much of his life.

Perhaps his organizing and mathematical mind enjoyed the way music builds patterns to arrive at order. Jefferson's recommendations for the curriculum at the University of Virginia included music as a basic liberal art. He defended the recommendations by coupling music with mathematical studies. Music eventually became a staple of liberal arts college curricula at universities during the nineteenth century.

Music unlocked the soul of this enigmatic and complex man. He had a compelling need

---

[147] Heinrich Heine, *Lutetia (Beriche aus Paris)*, from *Sämtliche Schriftten* (München: HG Klaus Briegleb Taschenbuchausgabe, 1997) 5:437. Translation courtesy of Mr. Hans Mueller.

to be surrounded by it. Nietzsche, a person more prone to venting his deepest feelings and one whose frequent illnesses led to much suffering, may have expressed Jefferson's feelings about music best of all. "Music," said Nietzsche, "is my lifeline…something for the sake of which it is worthwhile to live on earth…."

Ein Leben ohne Musik ist Irrtum!

(A life without music makes no sense!)[148]

---

[148] Friedrich Nietzsche, *Goetzendaemmerung, Brueche und Pfeile*, Vol. 8, Kroener Ausgabe #21, 459.

BIBLIOGRAPHY

Primary Sources

Abbott, W.W. ed., et al. *The Papers of George Washington, Presidential Series.* 8 vols. Charlottesville: UP of Virginia, 1987-1999.

Anderson, Emily. *The Letters of Mozart and His Family Chronologically Arranged, Translated and Edited.* 3rd ed. London: Macmillan, 1988.

Bear, James Adams, Jr., & Lucia C. Stanton, eds. *Jefferson's Memorandum Books: Accounts, with Legal Records and Miscellany, 1767-1826.* 2 vols. Princeton: Princeton UP, 1997. [*"Memorandum & Account Books"*]

Betts, Edwin Morris, and James Adams Bear, Jr., eds. *The Family Letters of Thomas Jefferson.* Charlottesville: Virginia UP, 1966.

Boyd, Julian P., ed., et al. *The Papers of Thomas Jefferson.* 27 vols. to date. Princeton, NJ: Princeton UP, 1950–. [*"Papers"*]

Coolidge, Ellen Wayles Randolph. Manuscript notebook of comments on H.S. Randall's biography of Thomas Jefferson, Alderman Library, Special Collections, U. of Virginia, n.d.

Goldsmith, W. Letter to Thomas Jefferson, April 20, 1807. Washington, D.C. Library of Congress, Manuscript Division.

Jefferson, Thomas. *Autobiography of Thomas Jefferson, 1743-1790 together with a Summary of the Chief Events in Jefferson's Life.* Introduction and notes by Paul L. Ford. New York: Putnam, 1914.

——, *Writings.* Selection and notes by Merrill D. Peterson. New York: Lit. Classics of the U.S., 1984.

Trist, Nicholas Philip. Memorandum, March 22, 1826. Nicholas Trist Papers, Library of Congress, Washington, D.C.

Wilson, Douglas L., ed. *Jefferson's Literary Commonplace Book.* The Papers of Thomas Jefferson, Second Series. Princeton: Princeton UP, 1989.

Secondary Sources

Adams, William Howard. *The Paris Years of Thomas Jefferson.* New Haven: Yale UP, 1997.

Bear, James Adams, Jr., ed. *Jefferson at Monticello.* "Memoirs of a Monticello Slave" [as dictated to Charles Campbell in the 1840s by Isaac Jefferson] and "Jefferson at Monticello: The Private Life of Thomas Jefferson" by Hamilton W. Pierson. Charlottesville: UP of Virginia, 1967.

Benson, Norman Arthur. *The Itinerant Dancing and Music Masters of Eighteenth Century America.* Diss. Univ. of Minnesota, 1963.

Betts, Edwin M., ed. *Thomas Jefferson's Garden Book, 1766-1824, with Relevant Extracts from His Other Writings.* Philadelphia: American Philosophical Society, 1944.

Boorstin, Daniel J. *The Lost World of Thomas Jefferson.* Chicago: UP of Chicago, 1981

Boyden, David D. *The History of Playing the Violin from Its Origins to 1761.* London: Oxford UP, 1990.

Bozen, M.M. *Letters of Mozart.* Trans. Hans Mersman. London: Dent, 1928.

Burstein, Andrew. *The Inner Jefferson: Portrait of a Grieving Optimist.* Charlottesville: UP of Virginia, 1995.

Burney, Charles. *The Present State of MUSIC in France and Italy: or The Journal of a TOUR through those Countries, undertaken to collect Materials for A General History of Music.* London, 1773. Facsimile Ed. Monuments of Music and Music Literature in Facsimile, 2nd Series LXX. New York: Broude Brothers, 1969.

Bush, Alfred L. *Life Portraits of Thomas Jefferson.* Charlottesville: T. Jefferson Mem. Fndn, 1962.

Butterfield, Lyman Henry, and Howard C. Rice Jr. "Jefferson's Earliest Note to Maria Cosway with Some New Facts and Conjectures on his Broken Wrist." *William and Mary Quarterly,* (Jan., 1948), vol. 5 no. 1:26–33.

Carson, Jane. *Colonial Virginians at Play.* Williamsburg, Virginia: Colonial Williamsburg, Inc., 1965—distributed by The University Press of Virginia, 1989.

Chinard, Alec Gilbert. *Trois Amitiés Francaises de Jefferson, d'après sa correspondance inédite avec Madame de Bréhan, Madame de Tessé et Madame de Corny.* Paris: Société d' Edition "Les Belles Lettres," 1927.

Cripe, Helen. *Thomas Jefferson and Music.* Charlottesville: UP of Virginia, 1974.

Ellis, Joseph J. *American Sphinx: The Character of Thomas Jefferson.* New York: Knopf, 1997.

Farga, Franz. *Violins and Violinists.* Trans. E. Larsen. New York: Praeger, 1940.

Farish, Hunter Dickinson. ed. *Journal and Letters of Philip Vickers Fithian, 1773-1774.* Charlottesville: Dominion Books, 1968.

Flesch, Carl. *The Art of Violin Playing.* Trans. Fredrick H. Martens. Boston: Carl Fisher, Inc. 1930.

Fleming, Thomas. *The Man from Monticello: An Intimate Life of Thomas Jefferson.* New York: Morrow, 1969.

Geminiani, Francesco. *The Art of Playing on the Violin.* London: 1751. Edited by David D. Boyden. London: Oxford UP Facsimile Edition, n.d.

Goodwin, Rutherfoord. *A Brief & True Report Concerning Williamsburg in Virginia.* 3rd ed. Williamsburg: 1941.

Heine, Heinrich. "Lutetia (Berichte aus Paris)" *aus Sämtliche Schriftten.* München: HG klaus Briegleb Taschenbuchausgabe, 1997.

Kimball, Marie Goebel. *Jefferson: The Road to Glory, 1743-1776.* New York: Coward-McCann, Inc., 1943.

——. *Jefferson: The Scene of Europe 1784 to 1789.* New York: Coward-McCann, 1950.

Malone, Dumas. *Jefferson and His Time.* 6 vols. Boston: Little, Brown, 1948–81.

McClellan, Edwin N. "How The Marine Band Started." *Proceedings,* U.S. Naval Institute, Annapolis, April, 1923, 581–586.

New Shorter Oxford English Dictionary. Oxford: Clarendon Press, 1973.

McLaughlin, Jack. *Jefferson and Monticello: The Biography of a Builder.* New York: Holt, 1988.

Menuhin, Yehudi. *The Violin.* Trans. E. Emery. Paris: Flammarion, 1996.

Moore, Ray and Alma, *Thomas Jefferson's Journey to the South of France.* New York: Stewart, Tabori & Chang, 1999.

Mozart, Leopold. *Versuch einer gründlichen Violinschule.* Augsburg, 1756.

Nietzsche, Friedrich. *Goetzendaemmerung, Brueche und Pfeile.* Vol. 8. Kroener Ausgabe no. 21.

Peterson, Merrill D. *The Portable Thomas Jefferson.* New York: Viking-Penguin, 1975.

Peterson, Merrill D. *The Jefferson Image in the American Mind.* New York: Oxford UP, 1960.

Pierre, Constant. *Histoire du Concert Spirituel 1725-1790.* Paris: Heugel et Cie, 1975.

——. *Thomas Jefferson and the New Nation*: *A Biography.* Oxford UP, London, 1970.

Randolph, S.N. *The Domestic Life of Thomas Jefferson.* Harper & Brothers, New York, 1871.

Randall, Henry Stephens. *The Life of Thomas Jefferson.* 3 vols. New York: Derby & Jackson, 1858. Repr. New York: Da Capo Press, 1972. ["H.S. Randall"]

Randall, Willard Sterne. *Jefferson: A Life.* New York: Holt, 1993.

Sadie, Stanley, ed. *The New GROVE Dictionary of Music and Musicians®.* 20 vols. London: MacMillan, 1980.

Shackelford, George Green. *Thomas Jefferson's Travels in Europe, 1784–1789.* Baltimore: Johns Hopkins UP, 1995.

Smith, Margaret Bayard, *The First Forty Years of Washington Society.* Gaillard Hunt, ed. New York: Scribner, 1906.

Sonneck, Oscar. *Suum Cunque, Essays in Music.* Freeport, NY: Books for Libraries Press, 1907.

Stern, Isaac with Potok, Chaim. *My First 79 Years.* New York: Knopf, 1999.

Storr, Anthony. *Music and The Mind.* London: Harper Collins, 1992.

Tyler, Lyon Gardiner. *The Letters and Times of The Tylers.* 2 vols. Richmond: Whittet & Shepperson, 1884-96.

Appendices

APPENDIX I

Agreement with John Randolph*

October [i.e., April?] 11th, 1771.

It is agreed between John Randolph, Esq., of the City of Williamsburg, and Thomas Jefferson, of the County of Albemarle, that in case the said John shall survive the said Thomas, that the Executors or Administrators of the said Thomas shall deliver to the said John 100 pounds sterling of the books of the said Thomas, to be chosen by the said John, or if not books sufficient, the deficiency to be made up in money: And in case the said Thomas should survive the said John, that the Executors of the said John shall deliver to the said Thomas the violin which the said John brought with him into Virginia, together with all his music composed for the violin or in lieu thereof, if destroyed by any accident, 60 pounds sterling worth of books of the said John, to be chosen by the said Thomas. In witness whereof the said John and Thomas have hereunto subscribed their names and affixed their seals the day and year above written.

JOHN RANDOLPH (L.S.)

TH. JEFFERSON (L.S.)

Sealed and delivered in presence of:

G. WYTHE,	P. HENRY, JR.,	Wm. JOHNSON,
THO'S EVERARD,	WILL. DREW,	JA.STEPTOE,
	RICHARD STARKE	

Virginia, ss.

At a general court held at the capitol on the 12th day of April, 1771, this agreement was acknowledged by John Randolph and Thomas Jefferson, parties thereto, and ordered to be recorded.

Teste,

BEN. WALLER, C. C. CUR.

---

*Julian P. Boyd, ed. *The Papers of Thomas Jefferson* (Princeton: Princeton UP, 1950)1: 66-7.

Appendix 2

Jefferson's Catalogue of 1783
Section 5, "Music"*

Chap. 35. Theory.
• Holden's essay towards a rational system of music.
• Jackson's scheme of sounds with the preliminary discourse.
• The same.
• Bremner's rudiments of music.
• Burney's present state of music in Italy
• Burney's present state of music in Germany
• Burney's history of music.
• Geminiani's art of playing the violin
• Geminiani's rules for playing in taste
• Heck's art of playing the harpsichord
• Compleat tutor for the harpsichord.
• Pasquali's art of fingering the harpsichord.
• Pasquali's Thorough bass made easy
• Zuccari's method of playing Adagios
• Miss Ford's instructions for playing on the musical glasses.
• Compleat tutor for the German flute.
• Hoegi's tabular system of minuets.
• Rivoluzioni del teatro musicale Italiano. dal Arteaga. 3 vols

Chap. 36 Vocal
• La buona figliuola del Piccini
• Alfred, a masque
• Artaxerxes
• Love in a Village
• Thomas and Sally
• The Padlock
• The Deserter
• The Beggar's Opera
• Handel's Alexander's feast, the words by Dryden
• Handel's Coronation anthems
• Handel's Funeral anthems
• Stabat mater by Pergolesi
• Pope's ode by the same
• Henry Purcell's Harmonia sacra. 2.v.
• Daniel Purcell's psalms set for the organ.
• Playford's book of psalms
• Purcell's 50 psalms set to Music
• The [?] companion, a collection of hymns and anthems.
• Butt's miscellany of sacred music.
• Purcell's Orpheus Britannicus.
• The same.
• Howard. British Orpheus. 6 books

- Clio & Euterpe. 3. v.
- Arne's Lyric harmony, op. 4th.
- Arne's Select English songs, 9 books.
- Baildon's Laurel 2d book.
- Hayden's Cantatas.
- Pasquali's songs.
- Jackson's songs.
- Drinking songs. 2 books
- Curtis's Jessamine
- Bach's songs 2d collection
- Heron's songs books 4th & 5th
- Favorite songs published by Bremner
- Dibdon's songs
- Book of songs
- Book of songs

Chapt. 37 Instrumental
- Corelli's concertos in parts.
- Vivaldi's concertos in parts.
- 12 Concertos chosen from the works of Vivaldi. 1st part.
- Vivaldi's Cuckoo & Extravaganza
- Hasse's grand Concerto
- Pergolesi's Overtures
- Handel's 60 overtures from all his Operas and Oratorios, 8 parts
- E. of Kelly's Overtures in 8 parts, Op. 1 (2d violin wanting)
- Arne's Clarke's Lampe's medley overtures in parts
- Abel's overtures in 8 parts, op. 1
- Howard's Overtures in the Amorous goddess in parts.
- Corelli's Sonatas.
- Cooke, 4 operas 4 parts. Also in 3 parts. 3 vols.
- Corelli's Sonatas op. 7th
- Lampugnani's Sonatas op. 1 in 4 vols.
- Corelli's Sonatas. 4 operas
- Pasquali's 12 Sonatas in 2 sets
- Humphries' Sonatas
- Corelli's 6 Sonatas, Op. 3
- Martini of Milan's Sonatas. Op. 1. 2. 3. 4.
- Abel Overtures Op. 1 in 3 parts
- Lampugnani's Sonatas.
- Giardini's 6 trios, op. 17.
- Campioni's Sonatas Op. 1. 2. 3. 4. 5. 6. 7.
- Humble's Sonatas
- Boccherini's Sonatas op. 2. 11.
- Gasparini's Sonatas.
- Kammel, Vanhall, & Schwindel M.S. Sonatas
- Campioni's 6. duets.
- Roeser's 6 duets, op. 2
- Godwin's 6 duets.

- Tessarini's duets, op. 2
- Bezossi's duets.
- Martini of Milan's duets op. 4. 7. 10.
- Battino's duets
- Figlio's nocturnes
- Figlio's duets
- Campioni's duets op. 8
- Degiardino's duets op. 2. 13. 3 v.
- Campioni's Sonatas, viz.
  op. 1. Paris
  1. 3. 5. 6. London
  6. Amsterdam
  7. London
  Duets.

Sonatas
- Abel op. 1st
- Agrel 3d
- Boccherini 2d and 11th
- Gasparini
- Giardini 17th
- Haydn 1st. 2d. 3d. 47th. 48th
- Humble
- Just. 8th
- Kammel. 5th
- Lampugnani 1st.
- Lampugnani & Martini. 2d.
- Martini. 1st.
- Pugnani. 10th
- Schwindel, Kammel, Vanhall

Concertos, Sinfonias.
- Corelli. 6th
- Haydn. 51st-52d.
- Kelly
- Pleyel 5th and 6th.
- Valentine.
- Vivaldi.

Duets
- Borghi op. 4th
- Chinzer 2d
- Godwin
- Haydn 9th
- Martini 5th
- Roeser 2d

Single parts
• Corelli 6th
• Vivaldi
• Corelli's Solos by Cooke.
• Corelli's Solos, op. 5
• Vivaldi's Solos, op. 2
• Tessarini's solos, op. 2
• Wodizka's solos.
• Campioni's & Chabran's solos.
• Geminiani's 12. solos, op. 1.
• Degiardino's 12. solos.
• Degiardino's 6. harpsichord sonatas, op. 3
• Burgess's lessons for the harpsichord.
• Boccherini's Sonatas for the harpsichord.
• Felton's Concertos, op. 1
• Stamitz's concertos for the harpsichord
• Bremner's harpsichord miscellany
• Hardin's lessons for the harpsichord.
• Abel's Overtures
• Periodical Overtures for the harpsichord.
• Heron's voluntaries
• Bach's Sonatas Op. 10
• Arnold's Sonatas for the harpsichord.
• Love in a Village
• Handel's lessons
• Lully's lessons.
• Felton's lessons.
• Stanley's solos.
• Geminiani's minuet
• Minuets, country dances, and several books
• Thumoth's English, Scotch, & Irish airs.
• Thumoth's Scotch and Irish airs.
• Pocket companion for the German flute.
• Pugnani's Solos, op. 3.

---

* derived from Helen Cripe, *Thomas Jefferson and Music,* 97-104.

APPENDIX 3

Collections of Jefferson Family Music*

- *Minuets with their Basses…for German Flute, Violin, or Harpsichord.* [London, ca. 1753].
- Manuscript music book containing a mixture of songs, hymns, excerpts from Corelli violin solos, minuets, and scales and preludes in all of the major and minor keys.
- *Stabat Mater,* composed by Sigr. Giovanni Battista Pergolesi. [London, ca. 1749].
- *An Ode–The Dying Christian to His Soul,* by Mr. Alexander Pope…adapted to the principal airs of the hymn, *Stabat Mater,* composed by Pergolesi. [London, ca. 1764].
- *The Anthem Which Was Performed in Westminster Abbey at the Funeral of Her most Sacred Majesty, Queen Caroline.* Composed by Mr. [Georg Friedrich] Handel. Vol. II. [London, ca. 1770].
- *Handel's Celebrated Coronation Anthems Three in Score, for Voices and Instruments.* Vol. I, [London, 1743].
- *The Psalms Set Full for the Organ or Harpsichord,* by Mr. Daniel Purcell, [London, n.d.] Several have the words written in, possibly in Martha Randolph's handwriting. The book contains: "Canterbury Tune," "York Tune," "Southwell Tune," "St. Mary's Tune," "100th Psalm Tune," "Windsor Tune," "London Tune," "St. David's Tune", "119th Psalm Tune," "148th Psalm Tune," "113th Psalm Tune."
- *Songs and Duets* composed by Mrs. Cosway. 8 pages of short songs and duets in Italian, with harp accompaniment.
- *Seven Songs* by Francis Hopkinson, [ca. 1784]. Volume of several groups of selections, bound together:
- *The Harpsichord or Spinnet Miscellany…*by Robert Bremner. [London, ca. 1765].
- *Six Sonatas for the Piano-Forte or Harpsichord,* Composed by Sigr. C. E. [Carl Philip Emanuel] Bach. [ca. 1775].
- *Eight Lessons for the Harpsichord,* Composed by Giovanni Battista Pergolesi. [London, ca. 1771].
- *Variations for the Harpsichord to a Minuet of Corelli's, the Gavot in Otho* [by Handel], and the *Old Highland Laddie,* by J. Snow. [London, ca. 1769].
- *Six Favorite Overtures Adapted for the Harpsichord or Organ,* Composed by Christian Ferdinand Abel. [London, ca. 1769-75].
- *Six Concerto [sic], pour le Clavecin ou le Forte-Piano…*Composed by J. S. Schroetter. Oeuvre III. [Paris, ca. 1785].
- *Ouverture et Airs de Ballets D'Alexandre aux Indies,* by de Mereaux, arranged for Clavecin or Forte-Piano by the author[ca. 1765].
- Pasquali's method of tuning the harpsichord
- Sonata–Ferdinand Stoes
- Rondeau
- Sonata–Ernest Eixner [Eichner]

- "The Merman's Song" –Haydn
- Overture from *Alexandre Aux Indies* [by de Mereaux]
- Duke of York's March
- Chorus–des Voyageurs de la Caravanne
- "The Shipwrecked Seaman's Ghost"
- "Tis Not the Bloom on Damon's Cheek"
- "Black Eyed Susan," "Two Catches," "War Song"–from Moore, "Dulce Domum," "My Nanie O."
- *Quatre Sonates pour la Harpe*…by Nicolai [Valentino]
- *Trois Sonates Pour la Clavecin ou le Piano-Forte*…by Nicolai
- *Trois Duos Concertants pour le Clavecin on Forte-Piano*…by Nicolai
- *Sei Sonate de Cembalo e Violino Obligato* da Luigi Boccherini, Opera V, [Paris, ca. 1780].
- *Six Sonates pour le Clavecin avec Accompagnement d'un Violon ad Libitum* par Mr. Johann Friedrich Edelman, Oeuvre I, [Paris, ca. 1780]
- *Trois Sonates en Trio pour le Clavecin…violin et violoncello,* par Ernesto Eichner, [Paris, ca. 1780].
- *XII Solos for a Violin with a Thorough Bass for the Harpsichord or Violincello,* composed by Arcanogelo Corelli, [London, ca. 1740]. op. 5.
- *XII Solos for a Violin with a Thorough Bass for the Harpsichord or Bass Violin,* composed by Antonio Vivaldi, [London, ca. 1721]. Op. 2.
- *XII Solos for a German Flute, or Hoboy or a Violin with a Thorough Bass for the Harpsichord or Bass Violin,* composed by Carlo Tessarini, [London, ca. 1736]. op. 2.
- *Six Solos for a Violin and Bass,* Composed by Wenceslaus Wodizka, [London, ca. 1750]. Op. 1.
- *Six Favorite Solos for a Violin with a Bass for the Violincello and Harpsichord,* composed by Carlo Antonio Campioni and Sigr. Chabran, [London, ca. 1760].
- *"Overture" to Artaxerxes,* by T. A. Arne, [London, ca. 1790].
- *Haydn's Celebrated Overture*–harpsichord or pianoforte
- *Two Grand Sonatas, for the Piano Forte or Harpsichord, with an Accompaniment for the Violin*…by Ignace Pleyel, [London, ca. 1790].
- *Three Sonatas for the Piano Forte or Harpsichord* by Ernesto Eichner, [London, ca. 1790].
- *Bland's Collection of Sonatas, Lessons, Overtures, Capricios, Divertimentos, &c, &c for the harpsichord or pianoforte without accompaniment, by the Most Esteemed Composers.* London, ca. 1790-94 No. 21, Vol 2:
- Edelman's Sonata I, Op. 1
- Vento–Sonata No. 22, Vol 2:
- Edelman's Sonata I, Op. 16 Overture to *The Bastile*
- Edelman's Sonata II, Op. 16, No. 28, Vol 3:
- Pleyel's "Cottage Maid"
- Edelman's Third Sonata, Op. 8 No. 29, Vol 3:
- Edelman's Third Sonata, Op. 16

- Martini's Grand Overture to *Henry the Fourth* No. 38, Vol 1:4:
- Gluck's Overture–*Paradie ed Elena*
- Edelman's Sonata IV, Op. 16 No. 42, Vol 1:4:
- Overture *Oedipe à Colonne,* Arranged by Lachnitth
- Eichner's fourth Sonata
- Haydn's Grand Orchestra Sinfonie, adapted for Piano Forte or Harpsichord. With an Accompaniment for Violin by Rimbault, [London, ca. 1785].
- Haydn's Grand Orchestra Sinfonie…at the Nobility's Concerts. Adapted for Organ, Harpsichord, or Piano Forte. [London, ca. 1785.]
- *Concerto, pour le Clavecin*…by J. C. Fischer, Berlin and Amsterdam, n.d.
- "The Plain Gold Ring," "Buy a Broom," "I'd Be a Butterfly," "Let Us Haste to Kelvin Grove"
- Overture to *The Deserter*
- 12 pages of unidentifiable sheets
- *Pieces de Clavecin* par M. Balbastre, [Paris, ca. 1765]–a group of 16 short pieces
- *Trois Quatuors* de Mr. Ignace Pleyel….[Paris, ca. 1785].
- *Trois Sonates pour le Clavecin*…by Leopold Kozeluch, [Paris, ca. 1788].
- *Trois Sonates pour Clavecin*…by J. S. Schroetter, [Paris, ca.1785].
- *A Duett for two Performers on One Forte Piano,* by Sigr. [Muzio] Clementi, op. VI, [London, ca. 1786].
- *Six Sonatas pour le Clavecin*…par Jean Cretien Bach [Oeuvre V][Paris, ca. 1780].
- *La Chasse pour le Clavecin*…par Muzio Clementi, Oeuvre XVI, [London, ca. 1786].
- *Trio pour le Clavecin…Violon*…par Wolfgang Amadeus Mozart, Ouevre 16, [ca. 1775, Paris].
- Unidentifiable printed scraps and fragments, including six sonatas.
- *Trois Quatuors* de M. Ignace Pleyel. With Violin accompanyment by [Ludwig Wenzil] Lachnitth, [Paris, ca. 1788].
- *Ouverture de la Bonne Fille…arrangee Pour le Clavecin*…par L. F. Despreaux, [Paris, ca. 1785].
- "Le Carillon des Trois Fermiers," "Trio d'Azor," "Air des Trois Fermiers," "Rose Chérie de Zemire et Azor," "Air de Trois Fermiers."
- Unbound scrap containing two sonatas, or parts of two sonatas, by Edelman, Op. VII, for pianoforte and violin.
- *Harpsichord Sonatas* by Dibdin
- *Easy Lessons for Harpsichord*…by Wagenseil
- Three minuets by Graff, Toeschi and Tenducci
- Sonata by Pescetti
- Lessons by Giovanni, Rutini, Green, and Castrucci [London, ca. 1770-80].
- *Recueil de Petits Airs*…Darondeau, Oeuvre VI, [Paris, ca. 1785]
- *Recueil de Romances et D'Ariettes*…Darondeau, Oeuvre IV, [ca. 1785].
- *Recueil de Petits Airs de Chant*…Martini, [ca. 1770].

- *Le Tout–Ensemble, de Musique, pour le Forte Piano, ou Clavecin avec Accompagnemens par les grands Maitres de L'Europe*…[ca. 1786].
- Several pages of untitled manuscript music, inscribed "Maria Jefferson" at the beginning.
- Niccolai's Opera 3rd, Sonata III, IV, V, VI, [ca. 1785].
- *Six Sonatas*…by T. Sterkel, Opera III,[keyboard and violin]…[London, ca. 1790].
- *Sei Sonate*…[keyboard and violin]…Matia Vento, Opera II, Lyon, ca. 1785].
- *Quatre Sonates*…[harp, violin, bass]…M. Gros Oeuvre, [Paris, ca. 1770].
- Unidentified sonatas 4, 5, and 6, arranged for piano duet.
- *Six Sonates* …keyboard and violin]…Valentin Nicolay, Oeuvre XI, [ca. 1785].
- Concertos 1-4, op. XI-XV…Schobert [keyboard], [London, ca.1790].
- Sigr. *Joseph Haydn's Grand Orchestra Sinfonie as Performed at the Nobility's Concerts, adapted for the Organ, Harpsichord or Piano Forte*, [London, ca. 1785].
- *The Celebrated Overture La Chasse*,…Haydn, [keyboard] [London, ca. 1785].
- *A Concerto* [no. 3]…[keyboard and instruments]…J. F. Kloffler, [London, ca. 1780].
- *A Favorite Concerto*…[keyboard and instruments] by Vincent Manfredini, [London, n.d.].
- *The Celebrated Overture* [to Sinfonie II]…by Haydn [keyboard] [London, ca. 1790].
- *Three Sonatas* [keyboard]…by Mozart, [London, ca. 1786].
- *Sonates in Quatuor pour le Clavecin*…par Mr. Balbastre…Oeuvre III, [Paris, ca. 1780].
- *Six Sonates*…[keyboard and violin…Mr. [Muzio] Clementi, Oeuvre II, [Paris, ca. 1783]
- *Six Sonatas for the Piano Forte or the Clavecin*…by Clementi, Opus IV, [London, ca. 1783].
- *La Chasse pour Le Clavecin ou Forte Piano* par Leopold Kozeluch, Oeuvre V, [Vienne, ca. 1781].
- *Sonates pour le Clavecin*…Opera V, par M. [Johann] Schobert, [Paris, ca. 1785].
- *Sonatas en Quatuor pour le Clavecin*…Schobert, Oeuvre III, [Paris, ca. 1785]
- *Sinfonies pour le Clavecin*…Schobert,…Opera IX, [Paris, ca. 1785].
- *Sinfonies pour le Violon et Cors de Chasse*…Schobert, Opera X,[Paris, ca. 1785]
- *Six Sonates pour Clavecin Ou Forte Piano*…Jean Cretian Bach, Oeuvre XV, [Paris, ca. 1775-79].
- Manuscript and music book inscribed "Virginia J. Randolph." Several different handwritings. Contains: Overture to *Lodoiska* by Knetzer; Dutch Minuet; "Murphy Delany"; "Jack Lahn"; Variations to "Duncan Grey"; song by Lord Lytellton; "New Crazy Jane"; "Arietta" from *LaFausse Magie;* "Rural Felicity" with variations.
- Manuscript music book inscribed "Ellen Wayles Randolph, Eliza Waller, Jane Blair Cary." Several different handwritings and many unidentified pieces. Contains: "La Canonade" by Balbastre; "God Save the Commonwealth"; "Rise Cynthia Rise"; "Lullaby"; Sonata of Edelman; German Waltz.
- Many loose sheets of fragmentary manuscripts in various handwritings, a few pieces tied together with string. Contains: "Vedrai Carino"; "New York Serenading Waltz"; "Fin Ch'han del vion" from *Don Giovanni* by Mozart; "Aurora"; "Batti Batti" from *Don Giovanni* by Mozart; "Valse Hongroise"; several vocal exercises; Rondo de Paganini; Air de Ballet; "Charming Village Maid"; "There's Nothing True But Heaven"; Musette D'*Armide;* Air de

Danse de *Roland;* Sonata by Haydn; Duo de *Blaise et Babet;* "Ye Lingring Winds."

- Manuscript music book, bound but fragmentary, contains: Variations on Sicilian Hymn; "Life Let Us Cherish"; "The Knight Errant"; "The Portrait"; Hungarian Waltz; "Come Rest in This Bosom"; "The Ill Wife"; A Favorite Scots Air; Air in *The Battle of Marengo;* "The Waltz Cotillion"; "Fin Ch'han del Vino"; "De Tanti Palpiti"; "Merrily Danced the Quaker's Wife"; "Je Suis Lindor"–Air du *Barbier de Seville;* The Spanish Fandango; "The Haunted Tower"; Clementi's Grand Waltz; Overture of *Panurge* - Gretry; Overture de *Chimene;* Choeur de Voyageurs de la Caravanne; Air Lison Dormoit; "Home Sweet Home"; "There's Nae Luck About the House"; vocal scales and exercises; Bonaparte's Grand March; A Much Admired Waltz by Mozart; "God Save the Emperor"; "Lord Courtney"; "Gramachree"–with variations.

- New and Complete Preceptor for the Spanish Guitar, Philadelphia, publ. by John Klemm, 1827, sold at P. Thompson, Washington. "Come Rest in This Bosom"; "Where Roses Wild Were Blowing"; "The Gallant Troubadour"; "Comin' Thru the Rye"; "Draw the Sword Scotland."

- *Der Freischutz* (opera) by Carl Maria von Weber. Complete score, inscribed on title page, "Margaretta Deverell."

- Small manuscript music notebook of songs, in handwritings of Martha Jefferson Randolph and several others. Contains: "A Poor Little Gvpsy"–by Arne; "The Silver Moon"–by Hook; "Owen," a Welch Song; "Ellen Aroon"; "Flutt'ring Spread Thy Purple Pinions"; Air du *Barbier de Seville;* "Life Let Us Cherish"; "Song in the Stranger"; "Crazy Jane"; "When Pensive I thought of My Love"–from *Bluebeard;* "The Tear"; "Poor Richard"; "Ah! Gentle Hope"; "The SailorBoy"; "The Wedding Day"; "Dear Nancy I've Sailed the World All Around"; "M'ha Detto la mia mama"–by Martini; "Thou Art Gone Awa' Mary"; "Flora"; "A Prey to Tender Anguish"; "Psalm 148"; "Old 100th Psalm"; "Psalm 134"; "Psalm 57, verse 8" by Handel; "Psalm 146, verse 6" by Handel; "Psalm 42, verse 9" by Handel; "Easter Hymn"; "Sanctus"; "Lewis Gordon"; "Evening Hymn"; "The Mermaids Song," by Haydn; "The Blind Boy"; "Duke of York's March."

- Two pages of manuscript music and notes in the hand of Thomas Jefferson. Opening phrases of compositions of Carlo Antonio Campioni which Jefferson owned, inscribed "On this paper is noted the beginning of the several compositions of Campioni which are in possession of T. Jefferson. He would be glad to have everything else he has composed of Solos, Duets, or Trios. Printed copies would be preferred; but if not to be had, he would have them in manuscript."

---

* derived from Helen Cripe, *Thomas Jefferson and Music,* 105-128. Monticello music collection: Special Collections, Alderman Library, University of Virginia.

APPENDIX 4

Tickets purchased for musical performances
while Jefferson was American Minister to France*

Performance Date: 9/2/1784
Venue: Comédie-Italienne
Aucassin et Nicollete, ou Les moeurs du bon vieux tems, opéra-comique by Grétry & Sedaine; *Silvain, opéra-comique* by Grétry & Marmontel
Price paid: 18f
1:561

Performance Date: 9/4/1784
Venue: Comédie-Italienne
Zemire et Azor and La fausse magie, each an opéra-comique by Grétry & Marmontel
Price paid: 6f
1:561

Performance Date: 9/8/1784
Venue: Concert Spirituel
Works by Handel, Anfossi, Giacomo Rust, J. P. A. Janson, L. B. Desormery, J. L. Duport, & J. B. Davaux; demonstration od new sostenente piano
Price paid: 6f
1:562

Performance Date: 10/4/1784
Venue: Concert Spirituel
"Carmen Saeculare, oratorio by François André Philidor [attended with "Nabby" and John Quincy Adams]
Price paid: 6f
1:566

Performance Date: 4/3/1785
Venue: Concert Spirituel
Symphony by Haydn; other works by François Devienne, Abbé Lepreux, & several Italian vocal works
Price paid: 6f
1:580

Performance Date: 4/16/1785
Venue: Comédie-Italienne
Richard Coeur de Lion, opéra-comique by Grétry & Sedaine; *Les Deux Chasseurs et la laitière* by E.R. Duni & L. Anseaume
Price paid: 6f
1:581

Performance Date: 4/28/1785
Venue: Paris Opéra
La Caravanne du Caire, opéra-ballet by Andre Grétry
Price paid: 15f
1:582

Performance Date: 5/5/1785
Venue: Concert Spirituel
Symphonies by K.F. Abel and J.F.X. Sterkel; Maddalena Sirmen (violinist & composer), Etienne Solère, Joseph Schuster, & Abbé Lepreux.
Price paid: 6f
1:583

Performance Date: 8/15/1785
Venue: Concert Spirituel
Symphonies by Haydn & J.F. Reichardt; other works by Cimarosa, Sarti, Sacchini, J.B. Krumpholz & F.J. Gossec
Price paid: 12f
1:592

Performance Date: 9/26/1785
Venue: Comédie-Italienne
Blaise et Babet by N.A. Dezède & J.M.Boutet de
Monvel; *Lucile, opéra-comique* by Grétry & Marmontel
Price paid: 6f
1:596

Performance Date: 10/9/1785
Venue: Paris Opéra
Didon, tragédie lyrique by Piccinni
Price paid: 5f
1:596

Performance Date: 12/8/1785
Venue: Concert Spirituel
Symphonies by Haydn, Abbé Sterkel, Henri Riegel; other
works by Anfossi, Viotti, Jean Lebrun, L.B. Desormery &
Florido Tomeoni
Price paid: 12f
1:603

Performance Date: 12/25/1785
Venue: Concert Spirituel
[Christmas concert] Symphony by Haydn; works by
Piccinni, Salieri, Tomeoni, Henri Riegel & Rodolphe
Kreutzer
Price paid: 6f
1:604

Performance Date: 12/26/1785
Venue: Musée de Paris (benefit)
Violin works performed by by Mlle. L. Gautherot:
Viotti, J.B. Davaux & Josef Myslivcek; Mozart piano
concerto, Piccinni *scène,* air from Grétry opera
Price paid: 6f
1:604

Performance Date: 1/20/1786
Venue: Paris Opéra
Pénélope, tragédie lyrique by Piccinni & Marmontel
Price paid: 11f/10
1:607

Performance Date: 1/28/1786
Venue: Comédie-Italienne
Le Bell Arsène, opéra-comique by P. A. Monsigny &
L'Eclipse Totale by N. Dalayrac & A.E.X. Poisson de
Chabeaussière
Price paid: 7f10
1:608

Performance Date: 2/2/1786
Venue: Concert Spirituel
Symphonies by Haydn & F.A. Rössler; Piccinni air,
duet by Myslivicek, other works by F.J. Gossec, Paul
Alday & Julie Candeille
Price paid: 6f
1:609

Performance Date: 3/18/1786
Venue: King's Theatre, London
La Scuola de' Gelosi, opera buffa by Salieri & other
(instrumental and vocal) works by Sacchini, Anfossi,
Paisello, Mazzoni and Mazzinghi
Price paid: 10/6
1:614

Performance Date: 3/23/1786
Venue: London Pantheon
Unspecified by London newspapers but apparently
included "some favorite glees"
Price paid: 4/6
1:615

Performance Date: 5/10/1786
Venue: Concert Spirituel (benefit)
Haydn Symphony, Krumpholz, Cardon, J.B. Mayer, F.
Petrini, de la Manière (for harp); Clementi piano
sonata; other works by Sacchini, T. Traetta, & J.B.
Davaux
Price paid: 6f
1:626

Performance Date: 6/8/1786
Venue: Comédie-Italienne
Nina ou la folle par amour, opéra-comique by Dalayrac
& de Vivetiere; *Le Tonnelier* by N.M. Audinot, *Les
Sabots* by Sedaine & Duni
Price paid: 6f
1:629

Performance Date: 6/12/1786
Venue: Comédie-Italienne
La Bonne Fille opéra-comique by Cailhava & Baccelli
(orig. *La Buona figlioula maritata*, by Goldoni &
Piccinni*); Les Amours d'été* by Barré & de Piis (vaude-
ville)
Price paid: 6f
1:629

Performance Date: 6/15/1786
Venue: Concert Spirituel
2 Symphonies by Haydn; airs by Sarti & J.G.
Naumann; *symphonie concertante* by Davaux; oratorio,
Esther by Sacchini, harp works by La Manière, J.G.
Burhoefer, L.C. Ragué
Price paid: 6f
1:630

Performance Date: 8/13/1786
Venue: Comédie-Italienne
L'épreuve vilageoise, opéra-comique by Grétry &
Desforges; *Rose* by Beaunoir; *Le Mariage d' Antonio*,
opéra-comique by Lucile Grétry
Price paid: 6f
1:635

Performance Date: 9/8/1786
Venue: Concert Spirituel
2 Symphonies by Haydn; airs of A.F. Gresnick and
Giacomo Rust; oratorio, *Le sacrifice de Jephté* by P.
Deshayes; other works by Henri Berton & Franz
Lamotte
Price paid: 6f
1:638

Performance Date: 9/9/1786
Venue: Comédie-Italienne
"Arlequinade, Les Deux Billets by Claris de Florian;
Richard Coeur de lion, opéra-comique by Grétry &
Sedaine; *Le mariage d'Antonio* by Lucile Grétry
Price paid: 6f
1:638

Performance Date: 11/1/1786
Venue: Concert Spirituel
Symphony by R.C. Ragué; other works by Sarti,
Myslivicek, Leopold Kozeluch, J.C. Vogel, François
Petrini, A.F. Gresnick & Isidore Bertheaume
Price paid: 6f
1:642

Performance Date: 12/2/1786
Venue: Comédie-Italienne
Fanfan et Colas by Beaunoir (a revival of *L'amitié à
l'éreuve*, opéra-comique by Grétry & Favart)
Price paid: 6f
1:646

Performance Date: 6/16/1787
Venue: Panthéon (benefit)
Symphony by Alexandre Guenin: works by Anfossi,
Grétry, Paisiello, Sacchini, F.J. Gossec, F. Petrini,
H.F.M. Langlé, C.A. Vion, & J. H. Lavasseur.
Price paid: 6f
1:671

Performance Date: 10/10/1787
Venue: Paris
Demonstration of music for improved glass
harmonica
Price paid: 3f
1:683

Performance Date: 11/2/1787
Venue: Concert
Symphony by Haydn; other works by Viotti, Leopold
Kozeluch, François Devienne & J.F.N. Carbonel
Price paid: 6f
1:685

Performance Date: 2/2/1788
Venue: Concert Spirituel
Symphony by Haydn; other works by Sarti, Paisiello,
Devienne, J. Lefèvre, Henri Berton, Niccolo
Mestrino, C.A. Vion
Price paid: 6tt
1:693

Performance Date: 3/17/1788
Venue: Amsterdam
Unspecified concert
Price paid: 2f
1:698

Performance Date: 4/12/1789
Venue: Concert Spirituel
2 Haydn symphonies; Luiza Todi, mezzo-soprano:
aria from Piccinni opera, rondo by G. Giordani, other
works by H. Berton, J.L. Duport, & violinist Johann
F. Eck
Price paid: 6f12
1:729

Performance Date: 4/30/1789
Venue: Panthéon (benefit)
2 concertos by & performed by Johann Friederick
Eck, violin; vocal works by Sacchini & L.S. Lebrun;
sonata by & performed by by Cramer
Price paid: 6tt
1:731

Performance Date: 5/27/1789
Venue: Panthéon (benefit)
2 Haydn symphones; number of violin works & vocal
works by Viotti, S.D. Grosse, Giov. Giornovichi, violin performed by by Geo. Bridgetower
Price paid: 6tt
1:734

---

* James A. Bear, Jr. and Lucia C. Stanton. eds., *Jefferson's Memorandum Books: Accounts, with Legal records and Miscellany, 1767-1826*, 2 vols. (Princeton, NJ: Princeton UP, 1997). Volume and page number follow each entry.

APPENDIX 5

Facsimile of Jefferson's Account Book entry for September, 1786, showing change of hand-writing after he shattered his right wrist. Jefferson injured his wrist on September 18 (see entry below for "2 Surgeons"). He apparently wrote in the entries for September 4 through October 2 with his left hand after the injury occurred. Note particularly the entries for September 8 ("Concert Spirituel") and September 9 ("Italians"). The latter is for an evening at the Comédie-Italienne with Maria Cosway, where they saw three comic operas. "Petit" is the name of his vallet.

2. p⁰ French & nephew a bill drawn on me by Sⁱ° Ban-
     -nister pay⁰ for 240f which charge to Bannister.
  see post. Dec. 11.
  p⁰ Goldsmith for books 6f10
  p⁰ d⁰ for 19ᵗʰ livraison of Encyclopedie. viz

        for myself — —   24
  I. J. Madison   24
      D⁰ Franklin   24
      F. Hopkinson   -   24
      Ja⁰ Monroe   23
      D⁰ Currie   - — 23
                            142

3. p⁰ seeing gallery S⁰ Cloud 6f
4. p⁰ Petit viz.

	Aug. 21-25.	Aug. 26 — 31.
Kitchen exp - - - -	234ᴺ (29)	213ᴺ 2 - 6 (20) = 49
Office - - - - -	120-9-6	73.14.
petites depences - -	54-18	32.15
postage - - - -	41-1	4
washing - - - -		36-14
waggon & harness hire		86
Semurier's acc⁰		40.9
Marechal's acc⁰		17.19
	450 - 8 - 6	504. 13 - 6

1786.
Sep. 4. p⁰ for buttons 22f10. gloves 4f6
  5. p⁰ seeing the king's library 3f. Madrid 6f
  7. p⁰ seeing machine of Marly. 6f. the Chateau 6f
     p⁰ Petit towards dinner at Marly 12f p⁰ at Louveciennes 6f
  8 paid at Concert Spirituel 6f
  9. paid seeing Gardes meubles 12f — for books 3f10.
     p⁰ M.lle Guyard ▬▬▬▬▬ for picture. 240f
     gave Patsy 6f p⁰ at Italians 6f
  10 p⁰ Valade for a picture 96f
  13 p⁰ hire of Piano forte 12f
  14 p⁰ Charpentier for a press for M. de lafayette 96f — for clamps 12f
     p⁰ seeing machine 3f
  16. p⁰ seeing Desert 6f
  18. p⁰ two Surgeons 12f
  19. p⁰ Petit on acc⁰ 600f
  21. p⁰ clothes for Patsy 64f10 — lent Mazzei 36f
  22. p⁰ postage 106f17 — Petit on acc⁰ 93f3
Oct. 1. p⁰ Correillon engraving 27f d⁰ for picture 48f
     2. state of expences of September.

	Sep.1 — 9	10 — 16	17—23	24-30	
Kitchen exp	266-6-6	206-11	172-10	116-4-6	(28)(26)(22)(13)
Office	107-16	88-2-6	56-10	107-8.	
Pet. depences	206-15	- - - -	57-4	128-19	
Postage	49 - 3	- - - -	19-0	28-17	
	630-0-6	294-13-6	305-4	381-8-6	1611. 5-6

APPENDIX 6

Examples of specialized bowing patterns in Arcangelo Corelli's Sonata for Violin and Continuo, Op. 5 in d minor, "La Follia" (1700)

The Theme

Variation No. 5: Double Stops with skips

Variation No. 6: Détaché

Variation No. 6 (continued): Détaché mixed with legato

Variation No. 10: Martelé mixed with staccato bowing (on one bow stroke)

Variation No. 11: Double Stops

Variation No. 12: Wide skips across the strings

Variation No. 13: Martelé mixed with legato runs (a virtuoso variation)

Variation No. 17: Mixed bowing and double stops